INSIGHT COMPACT GUIDE

MOROCCO

Compact Guide: Morocco is the ultimate quick-reference guide to this fascinating destination. It tells you all you need to know about Morocco's attractions, from its kasbahs and bazaars to its beautiful beaches and towering mountain ranges, not forgetting the imperial capitals of Fes, Marrakech, Meknes and Rabat.

This is one of 130 Compact Guides, combining the interests and enthusiasms of two of the world's best-known information providers: Insight Guides, whose innovative titles have set the standard for visual travel guides since 1970, and Discovery Channel, the world's premier source of nonfiction television programming.

Discovery CHANNEL

APA PUBLICATIONS

Part of the Langenscheidt Publishing Group

Insight Compact Guide: Morocco

Written by: Ingeborg Lehmann
English version by: Susan Bollans, Alan Keohane and Dorothy Stannard
Photography by: Phil Wood
Additional photography by: Tony Halliday 6, 8, 9T&B, 20–21, 49,
   51T&B, 54B, 87, 90, 93T&B, 101T, 106B, 112
   Alan Keohane 12, 44B, 47, 54, 57, 61, 71, 79, 105 110, 111T&B
Cover picture by: Tony Page/Impact
Design: Roger Williams
Picture Editor: Hilary Genin
Maps: Polyglott/Buchhaupt

Editorial Director: Brian Bell
Managing Editor: Tony Halliday

CONTACTING THE EDITORS: As every effort is made to provide accurate
information in this publication, we would appreciate it if readers would
call our attention to any errors and omissions by contacting:
Apa Publications, PO Box 7910, London SE1 1WE, England.
Fax: (44 20) 7403 0290
e-mail: insight@apaguide.demon.co.uk

Information has been obtained from sources believed to be reliable,
but its accuracy and completeness, and the opinions based thereon,
are not guaranteed.

© 2002 APA Publications GmbH & Co. Verlag KG Singapore Branch, Singapore.

First Edition 1999. Second Edition 2002
Printed in Singapore by Insight Print Services (Pte) Ltd
Original edition © Polyglott-Verlag Dr Bolte KG, Munich

Worldwide distribution enquiries:
APA Publications GmbH & Co. Verlag KG (Singapore Branch)
38 Joo Koon Road, Singapore 628990
Tel: (65) 865 1600, Fax: (65) 861-6438

Distributed in the UK & Ireland by:
GeoCenter International Ltd
The Viables Centre, Harrow Way, Basingstoke,
Hampshire RG22 4BJ
Tel: (44 1256) 817 987, Fax: (44 1256) 817-988

Distributed in the United States by:
Langenscheidt Publishers, Inc.
46–35 54th Road, Maspeth, NY 11378
Tel: (1 718) 784 0055, Fax: (1 718) 784 0640

www.insightguides.com

MOROCCO

Introduction

Places

Culture

Travel Tips

▷ **The Atlas Mountains (p93)** Snow-capped mountains meet the desert along the stunning Valley of the Thousand kasbahs.

△ **Volubilis (p41)** The Roman site of Volubilis, northwest of Meknes, has many beautiful mosaics *in situ*.

△ **Aït Benhaddou (p102)** This dramatic *pisé* village has been the setting for many cinema epics.

◁ **Essaouira (p61)** Coastal Essaouira is a great place to unwind.

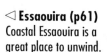

△ **Meknes (p34)** Tiled detail in this vast imperial city built by Sultan Moulay Ismail.

◁ **Fes (p41)** Fes is packed with medieval mosques, *madrassas* and *fondouks*. At its centre is the Karaouiyne Mosque.

△ **Tafraoute (p69)**
High up in the Anti Atlas, villagers of Tafraoute take visitors on walking tours of this spectacular almond-growing region.

▽ **Rabat (p22)**
The attractive capital of Morocco has several ancient monuments, including the 12th-century Tour Hassan, built by the Almohads.

▽ **Desert dunes (p91)**
Expeditions into the sand dunes of Erg Chebbi, the highest in Morocco, can be arranged from Erfoud in the Tafilalet.

△ **Marrakech (p52)**
The labyrinthine souks of Marrakech are crammed with wonderful things to buy, from silk slippers and spices to fabulous carpets and tessellated tables.

Flavours of the Orient

Wherever you go in Morocco, you will be assailed by a range and intensity of impressions that few countries so close to Europe can match. From the long Atlantic beaches and the rocky coves of the Mediterranean to the rugged mountains of the Rif, from the remoter peaks of the High and Middle Atlas to the desert sands and plains of the south, this is a dramatically beautiful country that constantly stimulates the senses.

In the ancient medinas of the imperial cities of Meknes, Fes and Marrakech the aroma of spices, fresh mint, newly baked bread and wood-shavings hangs in the air; strong colours dazzle the eyes, and the sound of the smithies' hammers resounds through the alleyways. South of the Atlas, bordering the Sahara, ancient battlemented kasbahs crown date-palm oases, evidence of the wealth once derived from the trans-Saharan caravan trade. Thriving modern cities such as Rabat, the seat of government, and the economic centre of Casablanca complete the picture.

Kingdom of Morocco
The history of a united Morocco begins in the 8th century with the establishment of the Idrissid state by Moulay Idriss I, a fugitive from the Abbasid Caliphate in Baghdad. After he was assassinated by the Abbasids in 791, his son Moulay Idriss II moved to Fes, then a rural encampment, and established the city, aided by immigrants from Spain and Tunisia. In the 12th century, the Berber Amoravide and Almohad dynasties extended the kingdom to include most of the rest of northwest Africa and Spain.

EAST MEETS WEST

For Europeans, Morocco is the gateway to the orient. But Maghreb, the name given to this part of North Africa, actually means the west, or literally 'the place where the sun sets', as indeed it is for the people of Arabia and the Middle East. For the inhabitants of the rest of the Maghreb, the Libyans, Tunisians and Algerians, Morocco is *Maghreb El Aksa*, the far west, the western outpost of the Islamic sphere.

In Morocco, Islamic civilisation merged with ancient Berber traditions, and the magnificent buildings of the sultans were not purely oriental but constructed in the Hispano-Moorish style. Morocco's unique cultural legacy is the result of numerous influences.

Compared with many other African states, Morocco is not a poor country. Its economy is developing at an outstanding rate, leading to the development of a middle class with a disposable

Opposite: inside a carpet-maker's home
Below: colours and flavours

income. Here, the traditional and the modern have always complemented one another. Moroccans are proud of the so-called 'golden mean' that governs their approach to life, in contrast to neighbouring Algeria, where Islamic extremists have been the cause of violence and economic isolation.

POSITION AND LANDSCAPE

Morocco is a large country covering some 518,000 sq km (200,000 sq miles) excluding the disputed Western Sahara *(see page 17)*. Bordering both the Mediterranean and Atlantic, it has an extensive coastline, a rich coastal plain in the north, forested mountains in the Rif and Middle Atlas, a huge alpine range in the Atlas (with more peaks over 3,000 metres/9,000 ft than the whole of the European Alps) and a southern border that extends into the Sahara Desert.

CLIMATE AND WHEN TO VISIT

The heart of Morocco, like southern Europe, belongs to the temperate climatic zone and has dry summers and wet winters. The southern edge with the Western Sahara marks the transition to a desert climate. The Rif and the Middle and High Atlas and Anti-Atlas also affect the regional microclimate and are responsible for the large temperature variations in the interior.

The Atlantic coast is generally cooler than the Mediterranean coast, and significantly cooler than inland. In summer, the collision of cool sea air and warmer air can produce heavy mists along the Atlantic coast. Dark rain clouds frequently pile up in front of the ranges of the Middle and High Atlas, ensuring good agricultural soil for the farmers in the valleys. On the north and northwest slopes heavy showers can occur outside the rainy season (November to March), resulting in flash floods that are sometimes devastating. Winter brings heavy snowfalls in the high mountains, and passes are frequently closed as a consequence.

Well Placed

Morocco is of great strategic importance because of its position on the northwest corner of Africa, which gives it control of half the Straits of Gibraltar and thus the entrance to the Mediterranean.

Oasis in the Dra Valley

The best times to visit Morocco are late spring and early autumn, when all regions are comfortably warm. In summer in the interior and on the southeastern high plateau the thermometer climbs to an average 30°C (86°F); cooler coastal areas at this time are perfect for swimming, with temperatures of 22–25°C (72–77°F).

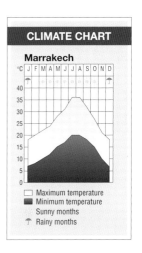

CLIMATE CHART

Marrakech

- ☐ Maximum temperature
- ■ Minimum temperature
- Sunny months
- ☂ Rainy months

WILDLIFE

Morocco once boasted a wide array of wildlife on account of its varied landscape and climate and geographical position, straddling both the temperate zones of Europe and the more tropical zones of Africa. Lions were common up until the early decades of the 20th century, cheetah were hunted in the south during the Protectorate era, gazelle were abundant, and even crocodiles survived in the Oued Draa up until the 1930s. Leopards are also believed to have survived in the remoter areas of the High and Middle Atlas until the 1930s.

Today, the larger mammals have either become extinct or are very rare due to declining habitats and indiscriminate hunting. Hunting parties of Gulf Arabs, for example, are mercilessly exterminating the last herds of gazelle.

The Moroccan authorities, with World Bank and European Union funding, are belatedly investing

Below: sand fish
Bottom: camels in the Dades Valley

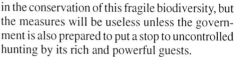

The bald ibis
The bald ibis is Morocco's rarest bird. Extinct elsewhere in the world, the species has been reduced to a small number of breeding pairs found only on the coast near Tamri north of Agadir and in the Oued Massa Reserve, 51km (32 miles) south of Agadir. Though created specifically to protect the bald ibis, the reserve attracts thousands of other aquatic birds, both resident and migratory. It also provides a home for wild boar, otters and jackals.

Below: prickly pears
Bottom: ripening dates

in the conservation of this fragile biodiversity, but the measures will be useless unless the government is also prepared to put a stop to uncontrolled hunting by its rich and powerful guests.

Nonetheless, Dorcas and Cuviers gazelle, jackals, a few striped hyena, honey badgers, foxes, fennecs, wild boar, mountain goats and even lynx are still found in remote areas.

The country's birdlife is generally in better shape. Morocco is home to a wide range of resident species and plays host to thousands of migratory birds that fly over in the spring and autumn or come to winter here from Europe.

Unfortunately, the large raptors are in danger; the last of the Bearded vultures disappeared from the High Atlas in the late 1980s, and the Egyptian and Griffon vultures are now thought to be extinct in Morocco.

VEGETATION

Morocco's once vast forests have been greatly reduced by logging, although great stands of cedars and pine trees are still found in the Rif and Middle Atlas. In areas with more than 600mm (24 ins) of annual rainfall, the most common trees are holm and cork oaks, cedars, juniper, thujas (cypress family) and various conifers, while in the Anti-Atlas the argan (oil is extracted from the

kernel of its fruit) predominates. In the southern coastal region, large areas are covered with Moroccan ironwood and jujubes, a fruit tree. Across the mountains in the semi-desert areas, vegetation is sparse; in the northeast Spanish grass with its rush-like leaves is dominant. The most common plant in the oases north of the Sahara is the date palm.

In order to protect endangered plants and animals, Morocco has created several national parks and reserves. There are five designated wetland reserves, four of which are considered of international importance.

POPULATION

Morocco stands out as a country where a wide variety of ethnic groups and tribes coexist without conflict. The population is around 30 million, including some 60,000 foreigners, mainly French and Spanish. In spite of reduced birthrates in recent years, 40 percent of the population is under 15 years old, but the government hopes that a further reduction in population growth (from 4.2 children to two children per family) will take place as a result of increased family planning.

Broadly, Moroccans may be divided into urban and rural populations, with many Moroccans of mixed Berber and Arab ancestry. The Berbers are the indigenous Moroccans. Their origins, however, are uncertain; theories include the possibility of European derivations, probably based on the not unusual occurrence of fair skin and blue or green coloured eyes. They are of three main types (subdivided into countless tribes): the Riffians of the north; the Chleuhs from the Middle and High Atlas; and the Soussi, found in the southwest.

Around 40 percent of Moroccans still speak one of the three Berber dialects – Tamazight, Tachelait and Tarifit – as their mother tongue. In areas that are predominantly Berber, it is often only the men who are able to communicate in Arabic. Berber remains incomprehensible to most Arabs.

When, from the 7th century onwards, waves of

Argan trees
Travellers in the region around Essaouira and Agadir are bound to notice thorny argan trees – often with a goat or two high up in the branches nibbling the leaves. Argan oil, derived from the tree's fruit, is similar to olive oil but has a distinct flavour. On its own or mixed with almonds as a kind of almond-butter, it is frequently sold by the roadside. Outside Morocco you can find it in specialist food shops and larger supermarkets.

Young woman in El Jadida

Who are the Berbers?

The Berbers in their own language refer to themselves as the *Amaziah* (the Free People). They are not only the indigenous population of Morocco, but of the whole of the region, from the Liwa oasis in Egypt to the Canary Islands off the Atlantic Coast of Morocco. It is a huge ethnic group, with an estimated population of some 20 million, linked by a common culture and language of Hamaritic origin (unlike semitic Hebrew or Arabic), split into several dialects with its own alphabet – *tifinah*. The latter is still used by the Tuareg of the Sahara.

Prayers in the High Atlas

Islamic conquerors swept across the Maghreb to spread the divine revelations entrusted to the Prophet Mohammed, the Berbers of the north embraced Islam, becoming fanatical adherents (though they retained elements of pagan pantheism, still evident today in rural areas).

Indeed, it was the Berbers who led the Muslim invasion of Spain in the 8th century; impelled to spread the faith *besiff* (by the sword), they routed the Visigoths and initiated seven centuries of brilliant civilisation at a time when the rest of Europe was still in the Dark Ages. In secular matters, however, the Berbers remained implacable; their rebellious nature was strongest in the mountainous hinterland and the south, where outside influences failed to get much of a foothold until the French and Spanish occupied the country.

In addition to the Arab/Berber population, there are the Haratines, dark-skinned Moroccans, many of whom are descended from slaves. They are found all over Morocco, but especially in the oases.

The once large and culturally important Jewish communities of the cities have now shrunk to a total population of around 16,000. Jews originally emigrated to Morocco from Spain to escape the Inquisition, but at Independence in 1956 many Jewish families emigrated to Israel.

RELIGION

Over 98 percent of Moroccans are Sunni Muslim, while 1 percent are Christian (Copt) and 0.2 percent are Jewish. Religion penetrates all areas of daily life. It is not limited to the *Allahu akbar* of the *muezzin* calling the faithful to prayer five times a day, but affects everything from laws governing marriage, divorce and inheritance to matters of personal cleanliness and eating and drinking habits. Such laws are laid down in the Koran, the Hadith (the sayings of the Prophet) or are derived from the Sunna (the school of law governing the Sunni branch of Islam).

The King, who is the political head of the country, is also the *Amir almu'minin* – leader of the Islamic faithful in his country.

CUSTOMS

Family life is punctuated by ceremonies marking important rites of passage – birth, circumcision for boys at around the age of three, engagement and marriage (still in many cases arranged) and death. Added to these are local festivities in celebration of Islamic holy days, such as Aïd el Adha, the feast in honour of Abraham's sacrifice, Aïd el Fitr, celebrating the end of Ramadan, and Maoulid, marking the birthday of the Prophet.

One of the most important times in the life of a devout Muslim is the completion of the *haj* (the pilgrimage to Mecca), which should be accomplished at least once during a Muslim's lifetime. The journey is saved for over many years, and families will club together to finance the trip for ageing parents. Moroccans too poor to travel to Mecca will undertake a series of pilgrimages to local holy sites. Many of the *koubbas* (the white domed tombs of holy men) dotting the Moroccan countryside attract a steady stream of pilgrims. Often these are women coming to petition their favourite saint, bringing small offerings and binding their contract by knotting strips of fabric to the grille on the tomb. *Moussems*, annual festivals in honour of the more important saints, attract pilgrims from all over Morocco; they include those of Moulay Idriss I in Moulay Idriss and Moulay Idriss II in Fes.

Below: young Moroccans pose
Bottom: a horse dressed for a local moussem *on the coast*

THE ECONOMY

Measures such as the privatisation of state enterprises and a reform of the stock exchange in Casablanca have strengthened the economy in recent years, and are attracting an increasing number of foreign investors to the country. Morocco has traditionally looked to Europe to trade. Phosphates, citrus fruits, textiles, olive oil and tinned fish are the most important exports. Most goods are shipped from Casablanca, though a brand-new duty free port is being built south of Tangier.

Morocco is the largest exporter and the third largest producer of phosphates in the world. Unfortunately, this industry has declined in recent years due to plummeting world prices.

The main focus of economic development is on the promotion of agriculture through the building of dams for irrigation systems, and the development of exports and tourism. Fishing is also important. The waters off southern Morocco are some of the richest fishing grounds in the world; Morocco makes a good income leasing the fishing rights to European countries such as Spain.

The Moroccan press
Since the relaxation of censorship in the last years of King Hassan II's reign the Moroccan press has proliferated, with many new newspapers and magazine titles appearing each year. Nearly all publications are in Arabic or French, but a few are beginning to publish English language sections. Some of the most original journalism is to be found in women's magazines.

GOVERNMENT AND POLITICS

Many African states look with envy at the constitutional hereditary monarchy of Morocco, which since the early 1990s has become increas-

The King's Palace, Rabat

ingly democratic. With its elected parliament, multi-party system, trade unions, astonishingly varied press and capitalistic economic system, this is one of the most liberal Islamic countries.

The king is both head of state and commander of the armed forces. Legitimised by his direct descent from the Prophet Mohammed, he is also 'Commander of the Islamic faithful' in his country and, according to Islamic belief, has *baraka*, Allah's blessing, rendering him 'inviolable and sanctified'. Tremendous power is thus concentrated in the monarch as the highest secular and spiritual dignitary. In the 1980s, King Hassan II underlined his piety by having a huge mosque built in Casablanca, which was inaugurated in 1993. This project was enthusiastically supported by the people, who were visited by officials and asked to contribute to the building costs as a 60th birthday present to their king.

Although the constitution was subject to major revisions in 1992 and 1996, when the regions were strengthened by the creation of a two-chamber parliament, the king still appoints the prime minister as well as other senior government and military posts.

On succeeding to the throne on the death of his father, King Mohammed VI declared himself a supporter of social change (including increased women's rights) to improve the quality of life for ordinary Moroccans. One of his first acts was to dismiss the hard-line interior minister Driss Basri, a close ally of Hassan II.

Below: the national flag
Bottom: Mohammed VI acceded to the throne in 1999

ADMINISTRATION

Regional reforms increased the number of *wilayas*, the town prefectures with district prefectures under them. The other administrative units are provinces, divided into districts *(cercles)*, community associations *(caidate)* and communities. The *wilaya* is administered by a *wali*, the prefecture and province by a governor (appointed by the king), the district by a *chef de cercle*, the *caidate* by a *caid,* and the community by an elected chairman.

THE DYNASTIES

For centuries Morocco was split into two spheres: one comprising territory under strict control of the sultan, the *bled el makhzen* (land of government), mainly the plains and coast, the other the mountainous inland areas settled by the less loyal Berber tribes, the *bled es sibha* (land of lawlessness), which resisted subjugation and taxation.

The Berber and Saharan tribes repeatedly challenged the central powers in the course of Moroccan history. Three of the six Moroccan dynasties – the Almoravides, the Almohads and the Merenids – were Berber in origin, while the Saadians and the Alaouites, though Arab, also swept up from the Atlas or the Sahara.

THE COLONIAL PERIOD

At the beginning of the 20th century, a deep rift ran through the population of Morocco, making it almost ungovernable, and giving France and Spain a convenient excuse for setting up their protectorates. Thami el-Glaoui (1872–1955), a powerful leader of the Glaoua clan of the High Atlas, allied himself with the French, and in recognition of his services was made Pacha of Marrakech by the French Governor General. El Glaoui ruled over a large part of southern Morocco and even attempted to topple the sultan.

Below: a Moroccan emir painted by Eugène Delacroix
Bottom: fantasia outside Taroudannt, the one-time capital of the Saadians

Despite such allies, it was not until 1934 that the colonial powers succeeded in bringing about a temporary peace in the country. Until then their efforts had been hampered by violent uprisings in the Tafilalet and the Rif Mountains, the latter spearheaded by Ben Abd-el-Krim, a Riffian chief.

The French and Spanish developed the Western-orientated infrastructure that led Morocco into the modern age. Today, one of the most notable legacies of colonialism is the division between the medinas and the new towns in all the main cities, a separation ordered by Marshall Lyautey, the first French Resident General. Lyautey believed in the importance of preserving Moroccan culture.

Fit for a king
When Hassan II died he left behind numerous palaces and unofficial residences scattered around the country. Some, like the palace in Agadir, had cost millions of dollars to build and yet had never accommodated the king for a single night. His successor, King Mohammed VI, does not share his father's taste for palatial living, and has promised to turn the majority of his father's palaces over to the people.

THE WESTERN SAHARA

At independence in 1956, France withdrew but Spain retained Ceuta and Melilla on the north coast, which it had held since the 15th century (and still does) and Sidi Ifni in the deep south (which it relinquished in 1969). It also held onto the Spanish Sahara, its desert colony south of Morocco, until 1975, when Franco announced plans to give up the territory. King Hassan II immediately claimed Moroccan sovereignty over the area and launched the extraordinary Green March, during which 350,000 Moroccans armed only with copies of the Koran marched into the region and camped for three days under the guns of the Spanish Foreign Legion, which held its fire.

On 14 November 1975, the Spanish transferred the administration of the disputed territory to Morocco and Mauritania, but demands for self-determination in the former Spanish colony gathered momentum, fuelled by the Polisario Front, and a 12-year guerrilla war ensued.

In 1988 the United Nations engineered a cease-fire and proposed a referendum to settle the fate of the region. However, after more than a decade of stalling by the Moroccan government, the referendum has still to take place, and the UN is threatening to withdraw. Meanwhile *Saharoui* who refuse to live under Moroccan sovereignty face an indefinite future in refugee camps in Algeria.

HISTORICAL HIGHLIGHTS

From 8000BC The first Berbers appear in the area. They leave rock drawings of the animals common at the time.

1200BC Phoenician seafarers found trade settlements. These are later taken over by Carthaginian merchants.

146BC After the fall of Carthage, the influence of Rome spreads west through North Africa.

24BC The Berber king, Juba II, rules over the Roman province of Mauritania Tingitana from the capital Volubilis, near modern-day Meknes.

AD42 Direct Roman rule under Emperor Caligula.

253 Rome withdraws from northwest Africa. Vandals invade the north coast, followed by the Byzantines in 535, who introduce Christianity.

681 Muslim Arabs under the command of Oqba Ibn Nafi invade the country.

788 Moulay Idriss I, a descendant of the Prophet Mohammed, flees the eastern caliphate and is welcomed by Berber tribes in Volubilis. He founds Morocco's first Arab dynasty, the Idrissids.

807 Idris II founds Fes. Shortly after, Muslim refugees arrive from Andalusia and Kairouan in Tunisia, establishing Karouyine University, one of the first universities in the world

1061–1147 Sanhaja Berbers from the Western Sahara sweep northwards as far as Spain and establish the Almoravide dynasty. Youssef ben Tashfin makes Marrakech his capital.

1090 Almoravide invasion of Spain.

1133–1248 Atlas Berbers from the Masmouda tribe, enemies of the Sanhadja, found the Almohad dynasty. At its peak, their empire stretches from Spain to Tripoli, and represents the flowering of Moorish architecture.

1248–1465 The Merinid dynasty, founded by Zenata Berbers, a nomadic tribe originating in eastern Morocco. It establishes a chain of Islamic colleges (*madrassas*), such as the Bou Inania in Fes, and the Chella necropolis in Rabat. Portuguese and Spanish forces encroach on coastal cities.

1465 The Wattasids, hereditary viziers of the Merinids, usurp the Merinids. Rule eventually breaks down and Morocco falls under the control of local *marabout* (holy men).

1492 Fall of Muslim Spain. Muslims fleeing Andalusia settle in Morocco, in particular in Fes.

1554 Sherifs, descendants of the Prophet Mohammed, found the Saadian dynasty, the first Arab dynasty since the Idrissids. Christians driven out of the country.

17th century Barbary Coast piracy. The piratical Bou Regreg republic is formed at Salé, set up by Moriscos who have been expelled from Spain.

1664 The present Alaouite dynasty is founded by Moulay Rashid, descended from sherifs who settled in the Tafilalet Mountains in the 12th century.

1672–1727 Brutal but effective rule under Moulay Ismail in Meknes.

1860 The Spanish colonial towns of Ceuta and Melilla repel an attack by the Rif Berbers.

1873–94 Moulay Hassan is the last of the notable pre-colonial sultans.

1894–1908 Sultan Abdelaziz incurs vast foreign loans, leaving Morocco bankrupt and open to European encroachment.

1906 The Act of Algeciras recognises France's 'privileged position' in Morocco.

1912 The Treaty of Fes. Morocco is divided up between the colonial powers of France (which gets the lion's share) and Spain, which gets the region north of Larache. Tangier becomes an international zone.

1920s Thami el-Glaoui connives with the French, pacifying rebellious tribes in exchange for power and privileges.

1927 The Alaouite Mohammed Ben Youssef ascends the throne as Mohammed V. In 1953 he is sent into exile in Madagascar.

1930s/40s An independence movement centring on the Istiqlal Party emerges in Fes. Unrest is met by repression.

1956 Dissolution of the protectorate under pressure from the Moroccan people. Morocco declares its independence. Political leader is Mohammed V, back from exile since 1955, who changes his title from Sultan to King.

1961 Death of Mohammed V. His son, Hassan II, succeeds to the throne.

1963–67 King Hassan survives five different plots against him, the most serious of which are led by the army.

1975 The Green March. The King leads some 350,000 unarmed men and women to claim the Western Sahara (formerly the Spanish Sahara) for Morocco.

1976 Backed by Algeria, the liberation organisation known as the Polisario disputes Morocco's claims on the Western Sahara. Morocco's relations with Algeria deteriorate.

1988 Relations between Morocco and Algeria are restored. A referendum is promised to determine the fate of the Western Sahara.

1989 The old North African dream of pan-Maghreb unity is revived with the founding of the Union du Maghreb Arabe (UMA).

1992 The promised referendum in the Western Sahara is postponed by the UN because of accusations of vote-rigging. The referendum is repeatedly postponed through the 1990s.

1993 The Hassan II Mosque opens in Casablanca.

1996 There are tentative signs of increased democratisation. In a referendum in September, 99 percent of voters are in favour of changing to a two-chamber parliament.

1997 The Parliamentary elections result in a narrow majority for the Socialist Union of Popular Forces (USAP). Abderrahmane Youssoufi is nominated prime minister in February 1998 after more than 40 years in opposition.

1999 King Hassan II dies at the age of 70 and is succeeded by his son, Mohammed VI. The new king promises increased democratisation and better rights for women. He also sacks the hated interior minister, Driss Basri, and allows many exiled dissidents to return to Morocco.

2000 The United Nations launches the Arab world's first centre for human rights training and information in Rabat.

Map on page 24

Arriving by Train

If you arrive in Rabat by train, be sure to get off at Rabat Ville, not Rabat Agdal, a leafy suburb to the west. Rabat Ville station is conveniently situated next to the Parliament building at the top of Avenue Mohammed V, the city's main commercial spine. From here, it is an easy walk to a number of small hotels or a short taxi ride to the more upmarket options.

Tour Hassan

1: Rabat

Rabat (pop. 1.7 million, including the twin town of Salé) has been the modern capital of Morocco since 1912 and was the capital of the Almohad Dynasty in the 12th century. It is the home of the country's parliament and government departments. In spite of many poor suburbs, the city centre has a prosperous air. Lushly planted squares and boulevards are the setting for elegant 1930s-style public buildings, and at the northern tip of town, the Oudaïa Kasbah rises picturesquely above the estuary of the Bou Regreg river to face Salé on the other side. Inland to the west is the villa quarter of Souissi, where high walls conceal sub-tropical gardens with swimming pools.

HISTORY

The cliffs on which the Oudaïa Kasbah stands were originally the site of a *ribat* (fortified monastery) built in the 10th century by Berber converts to Islam. In 1150, the Almohad Abd el-Moumen built a kasbah with a mosque on the site of the ruined *ribat*.

His grandson, Abou Youssef Yaacoub el-Mansour (1184–99), moved the royal capital of his large realm, Rabat el-Fath (the Rabat of Victory), further south. The 6km (3.7 miles) of walls, fortified by bastions and five monumental portals, had only just been completed when he died. The square minaret of the unfinished great mosque, the Tour Hassan, is still one of the city's landmarks. The half-finished Rabat fell into ruin when succeeding sultans transferred the capital back to Marrakech.

In 1609, the city was resettled by Jews and Muslims fleeing persecution in Al-Andalus. When the kasbah became too crowded, they founded the present-day medina, protecting its south side with a wall. Later in the 17th century it was primarily these settlers who opposed the central power of the Saadians in Marrakech. They declared the independent 'Republic of Bou Regreg' and financed their state by organised piracy, which plagued the Mediterranean until the beginning of the 19th century.

The core of the Ville Nouvelle was built under the French as their administrative centre. Since then, it has expanded far beyond the Almohad walls, with suburbs sprawling east and west. As a capital, it is overshadowed by the economic metropolis of Casablanca along the coast.

CITY TOUR

All the sights of the inner city can be reached on foot, though you may want to take a taxi to reach the Chellah, which is a long, hot walk during summer. Independent travellers can find their way around Rabat without having to employ a guide.

Begin a tour at the city's chief sight, the 12th-century ★★ **Tour Hassan ❶**, which also serves as a useful orientation point. Abou Youssef Yaacoub el-Mansour, the founder of Rabat and the most important ruler of the Almohad dynasty, commissioned the building of a mosque in honour of victories in Spain at the end of the 12th century. It was to be the second largest mosque in the Islamic world, but when Yaacoub el-Mansour died, just four years after building had begun, the work was stopped and the mosque gradually fell into ruin, a process that was accelerated by a major earthquake in 1755.

Star Attraction
● **Tour Hassan**

Below: outside the mausoleum of Mohammed V
Bottom: the Chellah

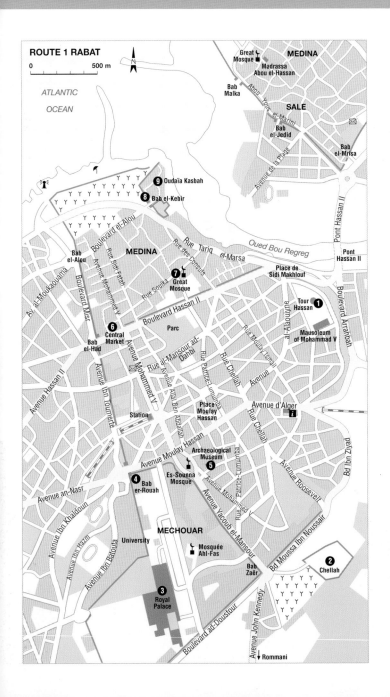

ROUTE 1 RABAT

0   500 m

N

ATLANTIC

OCEAN

MEDINA

SALE

Great Mosque

Madrassa Abou el-Hassan

Bab Malka

Bab el-Jedid

Bab el-Mrisa

Abou Yous el-Marini

Avenue de la Plage

Pont Hassan II

9 Oudaïa Kasbah

8 Bab el-Kebir

Oued Bou Regreg

Pont Hassan II

Bab el-Alou

Boulevard el-Alou

Rue Sidi Fatah

Avenue Mohammed V

MEDINA

Rue Tariq el-Marsa

Rue des Consuls

Place de Sidi Makhlouf

Boulevard Arrabah

7 Great Mosque

Rue Souika

Boulevard Hassan II

1 Tour Hassan

al-Alaouyne

Av. al-Moukaouama

Boulevard Misr

6 Central Market

Parc

Rue al-Mansour ad-Dahbi

Rue Moulay Ismaïl

Mausoleum of Mohammad V

Bab el-Had

Avenue Mohammed V

Rue Chellah

Rue Patrice Lumumba

Avenue

Avenue Hassan II

Avenue Ibn Toumerta

Station

Avenue Attai Ben Abdallah

Place Moulay Hassan

Avenue d'Alger

Rue Chellah

i

Avenue an-Nasr

Avenue Moulay Hassan

Archaeological Museum

5

Avenue Roosevelt

Bd Ibn Zaïd

4 Bab er-Rouah

Es-Sounna Mosque

Avenue Mohammed V

Rue Patrice Lumumba

Avenue Ibn Khaldoun

Avenue Ibn Hazm

Avenue Ibn Batouta

University

MECHOUAR

Mosquée Ahl-Fas

Avenue Yaooub el-Mansour

Bd Moussa Ibn Noussair

Bab Zaër

2 Chellah

3 Royal Palace

Boulevard ad-Doustour

Avenue John Kennedy

↓ Rommani

The square, reddish-brown minaret dominates the northern side of the site. Extending from here, a forest of columns is all that remains of the planned 19 naves of the prayer hall. The 44-m (144-ft) minaret was one of three similar towers built by the Almohads, the other two being the minaret of the Koutoubia mosque in Marrakech and the Giralda in Seville. Its stone relief decoration is an example of the elegant simplicity of Almohad art in the 12th century.

Opposite the minaret is the ★ **Mausoleum of Mohammed V** (open to non-Muslims) built between 1961 and 1971. The marble pavilion also contains the tomb of the late King Hassan II and his brother Moulay Abdallah.

MERINID NECROPOLIS

A rather long but pleasant walk takes you along Avenue Mohammed V, past the main ministry buildings, to the ruins of ★★ **Chellah** ❷ (open daily 9am–6pm). The complex lies outside the Almohad wall on the Bab Zaër and is also surrounded by a high wall.

The Carthaginians are known to have founded a trade settlement here in the 3rd century BC. Later the Romans built the river port of Sala, and from the 13th century the Merinids used the deserted area as a necropolis. It was only during the reigns of Abou Saïd (1310–31) and Abou el-Hassan (1331–51) that the enclosing earth walls were built; the massive portal has two turns, projecting bastions and stone reliefs in Kufic script.

Inside, the grave of the Sultan Abou el-Hassan is one of the most interesting, with artistic inscriptions. Nearby is the grave of his wife, Shams ed-Douha ('The Light of Dawn'), reputedly an Englishwoman. With its wild garden, the reddish minaret of the Merinid mosque rising out of the middle and the domed *marabouts* (tombs), Chellah has a rather poetic atmosphere. Storks, traditional symbols of good fortune, build their nests in the walls and trees, and the stone-lined pool in the *hammam* is populated by a colony of eels that are thought to confer fertility.

Map on page 24

Star Attraction
● Chellah

Funeral for a king
King Hassan II died at the age of 70, in July 1999, after 38 years on the throne. His funeral in Rabat was attended by an estimated 2 million Moroccans. In sweltering summer temperatures, dozens of heads of state, including the US, French and Israeli presidents, walked behind the funeral cortege from the royal palace to the Mausoleum of Mohammed V, a distance of 3km (2 miles). The king was laid to rest in a tomb alongside his father.

Mausoleum of Mohammed V

Map on page 24

*Below and bottom: guarding
the Royal Palace*

THE ROYAL PALACE

From Chellah, go back through Bab Zaër to the
★ **Royal Palace ❸**, built in 1864 and enlarged by
Mohammed V and Hassan II. The buildings, vis-
ible from outside, are roofed with the typical
green-glazed tiles; and palace guards patrol in
front of the ceremonial Moorish portals.

The **Bab er-Rouah ❹**, the 'Gate of the Winds',
now marooned on the busy intersection joining
Avenue an Nasr and Avenue Moulay Hassan, was
the most important entrance in the Almohad wall.
The monumental structure is lightened with beautiful Koran suras, arabesques and decorative
shells; the domed rooms of the gate complex are
frequently used as galleries for exhibitions.

Not far from here, tucked behind the Mosque -
Es-Sounna at the top of Avenue Mohammed V,
is the ★ **Archaeological Museum ❺** (Musée
Archéologique; 23 Rue el-Brihi; open 9–11.30am,
2.30–5.30pm, closed Tues). This national museum
contains archaeological findings from prehistoric,
Phoenician, Carthaginian and Roman sites in
Morocco. The highlights of the museum – bronze
sculptures from Roman Volubilis *(see page 40)*,
are displayed in the Salle des Bronzes (separate
building; the custodian will open it specially). They
include magnificent busts of Cato the Younger and
King Juba II. Juba II ruled Mauritania Tingitana
for around half a century until his death, in his

enties, in AD 23. He married Cleopatra Silene ('the Moon'), the daughter of Antony and Cleopatra, and was one of the most prolific writers of his time in Latin, Greek and Punic.

THE MEDINA

After a little window-shopping under the arcades along the Avenue Mohammed V, a coffee stop on the shady terrace of the Balima Hotel will be very welcome. At the bottom of the avenue, the **Central Market ❻** (Marché Central; closed Fri and Sun pm) marks the entrance to the ★ **medina**.

From here, Rue Souika, the medina's main thoroughfare for shopping, cuts east to Rue des Consuls, passing the **Great Mosque ❼** on the right. Built in 1882, the mosque replaced a previous building on this site. The top of its simple minaret was added in 1939.

In Rue des Consuls, carpet dealers try to entice passers-by inside their shops with the phrase '*pour le plaisir des yeux*' ('for the pleasure of seeing'). Rabat is a good place to buy traditional *ribati* pile carpets, which tend to come in strong reds and blues. Most are produced by sweated labour in factories, but private carpet-makers sell in the souk on Thursday mornings.

At the end of the carpet souk stands the ★ **Bab el-Kebir ❽**, the main entrance to the Oudaïa Kasbah. Yaacoub el-Mansour built this bastion on the highest point of the kasbah at the end of the 12th century. The most magnificent gateway to be erected during Almohad rule, it is splendidly decorated with bands of Kufic inscription.

INTO THE KASBAH

The ★ **Oudaïa Kasbah ❾** stands on the site of the 10th-century Berber *ribat* mentioned previously. The **Kasbah Mosque** dates from the 18th century, and replaced a building from the time of Abd el-Moumen (around 1150). Moulay Ismail recruited mercenaries from the Oudaïa tribe and stationed them in this kasbah. Its narrow cobbled streets, whitewashed walls and brown doors

The Oudaïa Kasbah

Map
on page
24

Café Maure
For sea breezes, mint tea and a traditional Moroccan pastry, adjourn to the Café Maure, signposted from the Jardins des Oudaïa. It is situated on the ramparts of the kasbah and its shady, rush-covered benches offer views over the estuary to the walled town of Salé.

Below: Musée des Oudaïa
Bottom: pottery in Salé

have immense charm. The **Jardins des Oudaïa** (open daily 8.30am–6pm), known as the Andalusian gardens, were added in 1915 by the French, but they blend harmoniously into the kasbah complex. The small palace, built on the north side of the garden by Moulay Ismail, has been turned into the **Musée des Oudaïa** (open 10am–5pm, closed Tues). The rooms display traditional arts and crafts, jewellery, costumes and musical instruments.

EXCURSION TO SALÉ

You can reach **Salé** (580,000 inhabitants) by *taxi collectif* (collective taxi) or bus across the Hassan II Bridge, or on one of the many rowing boats that ferry passengers across the river for a few dirhams. In the Middle Ages, the inhabitants of Salé conducted a brisk trade with European merchants, and the Moorish palaces still standing in the medina testify to their prosperity. From 1609, Salé was settled by *Moriscos*, Muslim and Jewish refugees from Al-Andalus, who established the independent corsair republic of Bou Regreg. They were the 'Salee Rovers' mentioned in Daniel Defoe's *Robinson Crusoe*.

Salé was also a centre of sophisticated craftwork, but with the rise of its rival Rabat in 1912, the town went into economic decline. Despite its prodigious current growth, it is very traditional and its inhabitants have a reputation for piety.

Among its most interesting cultural sight is the **Madrassa Abou el-Hassan** (open daily 9am–noon, 3–6pm), a theological college built by the Merinids in 1341. Its inner courtyard is decorated with bands of *zellige* (faïence mosaic), incised stucco and carved cedar wood; off the gallery, which is supported by 16 columns, are the cells in which the students lodged. A splendid view can be had from the roof terrace. Next door is the **Great Mosque** (closed to non-Muslims), founded by the Almohads.

In the former bastion of Borj Sidi Ben Achir, dating from the 18th century, is a small ceramics museum. Salé is known for its potteries, which are situated away from the town, beside the airport road out of Rabat.

2: Casablanca

Map on page 30

Casablanca, Morocco's economic capital, is a sprawling conurbation of about 3 million inhabitants. The reality of the city is a far cry from the Sin City portrayed in the film *Casablanca*, which was shot entirely in Hollywood. Since the end of the 1990s, the city has seen the rapid rise of new commercial centres around Zerktouni and Anfa boulevards and in the Maarif quarter, away from the old centre of Avenue Hassan II and the Avenue des FAR. The Twin Center, a pair of white skyscrapers, is the newest landmark and a symbol of the vibrant consumer economy that has gripped the country following liberalisation of import duties and the privatisation of the telecommunications and banking industries.

Below: street vendor
Bottom: old town battlements

For those with a disposable income, life has never been better; however, for the poorer classes, who make up the vast majority of the population, life has not improved, and the widening gap between rich and poor exacerbates the kind of social problems found in all large cities.

At least public awareness of such problems has also increased. Recent indicators of a new social conscience include Babil Ayouch's hard-hitting film *Ali Zaoua* about Casablanca street children, and a publicity campaign highlighting the plight of young domestic servants.

Map below

HISTORY

The elegant quarter of Anfa was originally the location of a Berber settlement of the same name, founded in the 8th century. Later, it became a busy trading port and also a base for piracy. While the merchants were engaged in the lucrative grain trade, the corsairs were just as successful plundering ships along the Portuguese coast. Piracy came to an end in 1468 following a devastating attack on its operation by the Portuguese fleet. In 1575 the conquerors constructed a new harbour and called it Casa Branca (White House). In 1755 the Portuguese were driven out, but by 1782

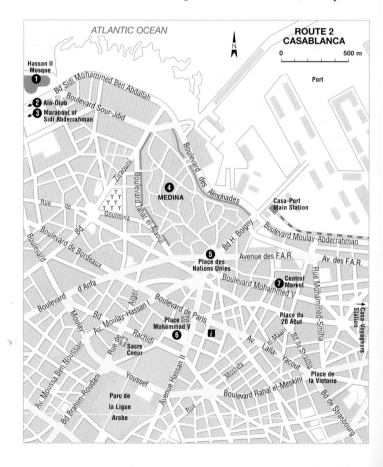

ROUTE 2
CASABLANCA

ATLANTIC OCEAN

N

0   500 m

Hassan II Mosque
1

Bd Sidi Mohammed Ben Abdallah

2 Aïn-Diab
Boulevard Sour-Jdid
3 Marabout of Sidi Abderrahman

Port

Ziraoui

Boulevard Talat el-Alaoui

Boulevard des Almohades

4 MEDINA

Rue   de

Goulmina

Casa-Port Main Station

Boulevard de Bordeaux

Boulevard

Bd

Bd H. Boigny

Boulevard Moulay-Abderrahman

5 Place des Nations Unies

Avenue des F.A.R.

Av. des F.A.R.

d'Anfa

Boulevard

Bd   Alger

Av. Moulay-Hassan I

Boulevard de Paris

Boulevard Mohammed V

7 Central Market

Rue Mohammed-Smiha

Casa-Voyageurs Station

Moulay

Rue de Rachidi

Place Mohammad V **6**

i

Place du 20 Août

Av. Moussa Ben Noussair

Sacre Coeur

Youssef

Avenue Hassan II

Av. Lalla-Yacout

Mostafa

Bd el-Maani

Bd el-Strasbα

Place de la Victoire

Bd Brahim-Roudani

Parc de la Ligue Arabe

Rue

Boulevard Rahal el-Meskini

Bd de Strasbourg

Spanish merchants were trying to take their place, renaming the trading post Casablanca (in Arabic Dar el-Beïda). An increasing number of Europeans settled here up to the mid-19th century, but many left following attacks by the locals.

Star Attraction
● Hassan II Mosque

FRENCH

In 1912 the first French governor Lyautey set about transforming the city into an international port and the economic centre of the protectorate of Morocco. Today, 59 percent of Morocco's manufacturing industry is based in the Casablanca area. The chemical, textile, foodstuffs and metal industries predominate. Greater Casablanca is the most populous part of the country, with eight district prefectures, and is the seat of the modern Université d'Hassan II.

Arabian nights
Casablanca offers the best nightlife in Morocco. A new, fashionable venue seems to open every couple of months, mostly along the Corniche or off the Boulevard Anfa. For a laid-back drink or two try the restaurant-bar Kasbar (7 Rue Najib Mahfound, Gauthier, tel: 022 20 47 47) or for more tempo try the Villa Fandango (Rue Mer Egee, Boulevard de la Corniche, tel: 022 39 85 08), one of the best nightclubs.

CITY TOUR

Impossible to miss, the ★★ **Hassan II Mosque** ❶ (Grande Mosquée d'Hassan II; Boulevard Sidi Mohammed Ben Abdallah; guided tours daily except Fri and on Islamic holidays) is the dominant feature on the skyline if you approach the city from the sea. Surrounded by water on three sides, the building complies nicely with the saying, 'Allah has his throne upon water.'

With this monumental building, Hassan II established himself in the eyes of the world as a champion of a tolerant Islam. Conceived for 105,000 faithful, it was designed by the French architect Michel Pinseau, and built by some 90 engineers and 30,000 Moroccan workers and craftsmen. It cost the equivalent of around £300 million to build, and as far as possible incorporates Moroccan materials – cedar from the Middle Atlas and marble from Agadir and Tafraoute. The earthquake-proof complex includes a *madrassa* (theological school), a national museum, several traditional *hammams* (baths) and an underground garage; from the 200m (660ft) minaret, a 30-km (19-mile) long laser beam points east across the night sky towards

Hassan II Mosque

Map on page 30

Mecca. The adjoining theological library is the largest in the Islamic world, linked by computer to other large libraries worldwide. Even the prayer room is high-tech: the electronically controlled sliding roof opens in only three minutes.

This is the only active mosque in Morocco open to non-Muslims (admission by guided tour only). Though the section of the interior open to non-Muslims is fairly small, it does offer the chance to see the work of some of Morocco's finest living craftsmen.

Below: the port area
Bottom: Aïn-Diab rock pools

AïN-DIAB

From the mosque, you can take a taxi along the Corniche to **Aïn-Diab ❷**, the coastal strip to the west of the city, which at night is bright with neon-lit nightclubs, restaurants, cafés and entertainments. By day, things are somewhat quieter: several sea-water swimming pools, built into the rocks by the French, make popular escapes for city dwellers during the summer.

Around 3km (1.9 miles) further on, crowning a rocky outcrop off the shore, is the **Marabout of Sidi Abderrahman ❸**. At high tide the tomb of the holy man is cut off from the mainland, but it is easily accessed by pilgrims at other times. The saint's *moussem*, a big festival in August lasting for several days, attracts large numbers of pilgrims from Casablanca and beyond.

THE MEDINA

The Americanised playground of Aïn-Diab is worlds apart from the busy **medina ❹**. All that remains of the old town, it is hemmed in between the Ville Nouvelle and the large fishing port. It has no historic mosques or *madrassas*, though there is an 18th-century fort, the **Borj Sidi Mohammed ben Abdullah**, overlooking the sea. But the medina is a hive of commercial activity, especially during the early evening, with heaps of different merchandise spilling over the streets, and it offers an interesting contrast to the slick New Town that overshadows it.

1930s ARCHITECTURE

Just outside the medina, the magnificent **Place des Nations Unies** ❺, overlooked by the Hyatt Regency Hotel, is both a busy traffic junction and the transition point between the traditional medina and the new town. From here, Casablanca's main boulevard, the Avenue Hassan II, runs south to **Place Mohammed V** ❻, the finest square in the city. Stylish administration buildings built during the 1920s, including the official seat of the *wali* with a 50-m (164-ft) clock tower and the Palais de Justice, surround a shady square with seats under tall palm trees. On the other side of the road, the monumental fountain (erected in 1965) is a magnet for pigeons and children – when it is operating.

Running off the Place, Boulevard Mohammed V, the main shopping hub before this shifted to Zerktouni and d'Anfa, is lined with decorative facades from the 1920s and '30s; look out for striking Art Deco grillework on staircases and balconies. The lively **Central Market** ❼ (Marché Central), just off the street, also dates from this period; dip inside to enjoy its larder-cool air and beautifully displayed produce.

Not far away, on Avenue des FAR (south and parallel to Boulevard Mohammed V), is the **Royal Mansur Hotel**; its ground-floor atrium bar is a pleasant place in which to have a coffee or beer.

> **Cultural corner**
> Casablanca has no official museums or galleries, but the ONA Foundation has established a private museum of contemporary art in a beautifully restored Art Deco Villa (open Tues–Sat 11am–7pm) at 30 Boulevard Brahim Roudani. The museum collects and exhibits contemporary Moroccan art, as well as hosting international exhibitions. Set in a spacious garden with a small coffee shop, it is a delightful place in which to experience a more contemplative side to Casablanca.

Place Mohammed V

Map
below

A corner of Meknes

3: Meknes

Meknes (pop. 530,000) was the capital of the second Alaouite sultan, Moulay Ismail (1672–1727). A ruthless but effective ruler who governed his country with an iron hand, Ismail is still admired today, and his imperial capital, renowned for its colossal buildings and enclosing walls which still dominate the city, is a popular destination for Moroccan visitors and foreign tourists alike.

Nestling in the countryside west of the city are two significant historical sites: the Roman ruins of Volubilis and the small town of Moulay Idriss, built around the mausoleum of Idriss I, the founder of the first Arabic-Islamic state in Morocco. Together these sites make a worthwhile day trip from Meknes, either by hired car, shared taxi or bus.

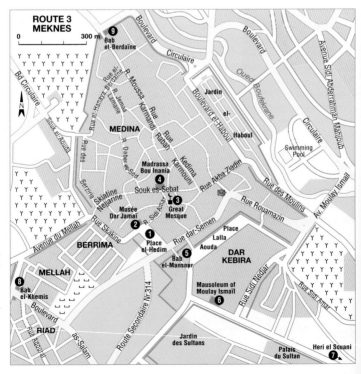

HISTORY

Though Meknes reached its zenith in the 17th century under Moulay Ismail, it was a significant town long before this. In the 10th century, Meknassa Berbers were attracted by the abundant supply of water, fertile agricultural soil and olive trees on the banks of the Oued Boufekrane. They called their scattered village Meknassa ez-Zitoun. Under the Almoravides, a fortified settlement was built on the site of the present medina, which subsequently acquired mosques, *madrassas* and wall fountains from the Almohads and Merinids. Viziers of the Merinid rulers, whose court was in Fes, had second residences in Meknassa.

The city's greatest period of prosperity, however, came under Moulay Ismail. This self-willed ruler raised the status of Meknes above that of the two royal seats of Fes and Marrakech and over a period of 55 years Ismail turned his capital into the largest fortified town in North Africa.

The scale of building was unprecedented. The palace complexes, built with stone plundered from the Roman city of Volubilis *(see page 40)* and the El Badi palace in Marrakech *(see page 51)*, reached giant proportions, enclosed by some 20km (12 miles) of walls.

After his death, the city declined as quickly as it was built, though the remaining ruins still give a good idea of its splendour and size. In 1912, the French founded a Ville Nouvelle on the opposite side of the river and established one of the most important agricultural and wine-growing areas in Morocco on the Meknes-Saiss plateau. Meknes is today an important crafts centre and the seat of the university of Moulay Ismail.

CITY TOUR

The medina begins at the **Place el-Hedim ❶**, a large square outside Bab el Mansour. However, before you plunge into its labyrinth take a look at the **Musée Dar Jamaï ❷** (open 9am–noon, 3–6pm; closed Tues), on the other side of the pointed-arched gateway, next to a pretty Moorish wall fountain. A long winding hall with a brightly

Tales of excess
Moulay Ismail's excesses are legendary. He is said to have had at least 500 wives and concubines, and of the many more children he fathered he had the girls strangled at birth and was not averse to slicing off the limbs of erring sons. To enforce his rule, he formed an army of 30,000 Sudanese soldiers who roamed the country keeping the tribes in check.

Place el-Hedim

Map on page 34

French connection
Moulay Ismail is said to have modelled his palace complexes on similar structures built for his contemporary Louis XIV in far-away France. He maintained flourishing trade relations with the French king, and even went as far as to ask for the hand of one of the French princesses, which was, however, refused him by the French court.

Nougat for sale outside Bab el-Mansour

painted carved ceiling ends in an inner garden. This was the house of the grand vizier Mohammed Ben Larbi Jamai, a dignitary at the court of Moulay Hassan (1873–1894). Jamai fell out of favour during the uprisings under Sultan Abdelaziz (1894–1908) and died in prison. The rooms display examples of regional arts and crafts, such as jewellery, ceramics and Berber carpets. On the upper floor, the private and reception rooms of the vizier can be seen.

THE MEDINA

From the peace and quiet of the museum you are plunged into the hustle and bustle of the adjoining souk. To the right of the fountain, a gate opens into the **jewellery souk**. The silversmiths of Meknes are traditionally renowned for their silver inlay work. Today there are only a few craftsmen who have fully mastered the art, and prices are accordingly high.

At the heart of the souk is the **Great Mosque ❸**. Its prayer hall is still lit by a chandelier inscribed with the name of the Almohad Sultan Mohammed en-Nasir (1199–1213). Moulay Ismail had the mosque renovated in 1695 and added the *minbar*, from which prayers are led by the *iman*.

In the midst of the noisy Souk es-Sebat, a pair of double doors with bronze reliefs open into a haven of peace and quiet, the ★★ **Madrassa Bou Inania ❹** (open daily 9am–noon, 3–6pm). Now no longer used as a Koranic school, the *madrassa* was built during the rule of Abou Inan (1351–58), who was also responsible for the college of the same name in Fes. Of the 50 student rooms, several have no windows, while others have tiny slits facing the narrow alley; only privileged pupils had rooms facing the inner courtyard. The refined decoration of the courtyard includes tile mosaics, plaster stucco work, friezes inscribed with Koranic suras and cedarwood carving. At the centre of the courtyard is a marble basin in the shape of a shell for ritual ablutions. The Moorish wall decorations are continued in the prayer hall, culminating in the frame around the five-sided prayer niche.

THE IMPERIAL CITY

Opposite the medina, south of Place el-Hedim, stretches Moulay Ismail's imperial city, concealed behind a 20-km (12-mile) long protective wall. The city comprised some 30 palaces, separated by gardens with pavilions and ponds, barracks, stables and an enormous storehouse. It is accessed via Bab el-Mansour.

The giant gate ★★ **Bab el-Mansour** ❺ has survived the centuries as the most impressive reminder of Ismail's reign. His life's work, it was completed by his son and successor Moulay Abdallah in 1732. Decorated with white marble columns and composite capitals from the Roman town of Volubilis *(see page 40)*, it is an imposing entrance to the imperial city.

THE MAUSOLEUM OF MOULAY ISMAIL

The mausoleum of the eccentric sultan was substantially enlarged by his Alaouite successors and restored by the late Mohammed V. Together with the mausoleums of Idriss I in Moulay Idriss, Idriss II in Fes and Mohammed V in Rabat, the ★★ **Mausoleum of Moulay Ismail** ❻ (Mausolée de Moulay Ismail; open daily 9am–noon, 3–6pm, Fri closed until 3pm; entrance free) is one of the most important shrines in Morocco. Beneath the canopy of the facade, the inscription translates as

Star Attractions
● Madrassa Bou Inania
● Bab el-Mansour
● Mausoleum of Moulay Ismail

Below: the Mausoleum of Moulay Ismail
Bottom: town transport

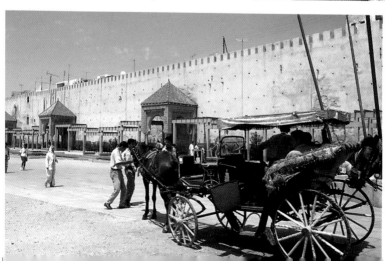

Map on page 34

Below: tilework in the Mausoleum of Moulay Ismail
Bottom: gates into the medina

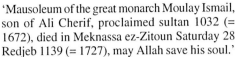

'Mausoleum of the great monarch Moulay Ismail, son of Ali Cherif, proclaimed sultan 1032 (= 1672), died in Meknassa ez-Zitoun Saturday 28 Redjeb 1139 (= 1727), may Allah save his soul.'

Non-Muslims may enter the mausoleum but must take off their shoes in the lobby. They can look into the lavishly decorated room containing the tomb. Above the sarcophagus, surrounded by a grille, is a 12-sided carved dome. Just off the mausoleum is a gateway to a cemetery containing the tombs of people who wished to be buried alongside this famous ruler.

HERI EL-SOUANI

The **Heri el-Souani** ❼ gives some idea of the gigantic proportions of Ismail's city. The storehouse, 180m by 69m (590ft by 226ft) and a good 12m (39ft) high, divided into 23 aisles by clay pillar arcades, was used for grain, while under the high vaults of the Dar el-Ma were cisterns 40m (130ft) deep, from which water was drawn by water wheels rotated by horses or camels.

Climb up the steps to the terrace of the building (now a pleasant café) for a panoramic view of the 400m by 100m (1,312ft by 328ft) Aguedal irrigation tank, the present royal palace and the ruins of the old Dar el-Makhzen, with the medina of Meknes beyond.

TWO GATES

Finally, mention should be made of two other gates in the wall. The **Bab el-Khemis** , the 'West Gate', dates from 1687 and originally opened into the garden quarter in which the ruler's viziers lived; at a later date the Thursday market was held here. The **Bab el-Berdaine** ❾ ('Gate of the Saddlers'), built in 1709, has ornamental bastions, diamond-shaped glazed-tile decorations and arabesques; it is passed on the ring road to Bab el-Mansour from the New Town.

MOULAY IDRISS AND VOLUBILIS

Numerous buses and collective taxis run from Meknes to ★★**Moulay Idriss**, 27km (17 miles) away. Built into the spurs of two hills, the town has grown around the shrine of Moulay Idriss I (788–793), founder of the first Islamic state on Moroccan soil. The most important holy site in Morocco, the town was out of bounds to non-Muslims until well into the 20th century.

Buses and taxis drop passengers just below the **Sahat Massir al-Khadra** ('Square of the Green March'), an attractive space with café terraces and a cluster of stalls selling nougat (a speciality of the town), nuts and votive candles. A few paces above here, a wooden barrier marks the beginning of the *horm* (holy area), which non-Muslims are not allowed to enter.

The sanctuary was given its present form by two Alaouite rulers: Moulay Ismail in the early 18th century and the extravagant Sultan Moulay Abderrahman in the 19th century. For a rooftop view of the sanctuary and the town, climb through the houses to the small platform outside the **Mosque of Sidi Abdallah el-Hajja** (a boy will show you the way for a few dirhams); the mausoleum complex is delineated by greentiled roofs.

ROMAN OUTPOST

Below the Zerhoun Mountains, 5km (3 miles) northwest of Moulay Idriss, lie the ruins of the

Star Attraction
● Moulay Idriss

Wine country
Meknes is the centre of Morocco's wine-growing region. Established by the French (though the Romans also grew vines in the region), the industry still flourishes, and you can now find Moroccan wines on the shelves of European supermarkets. The reds are considered to be better than the whites; look out for the rich and fruity Guerrouane and Vieux Papes. To buy wine in Morocco, go to an upmarket grocer in the New Town of a city. Alcohol is never sold in the medinas.

Barbecued merguez

Map
on page
34

Horse riding and more
Tijania Range (tel: 061 20 38 14 or 055 53 35 06) is set in the heart of Meknes' wine region, on the road to El Menzeh (in the direction of Boufrekane). The ranch is an Arabian horse stud, organic farm and country restaurant offering entirely home-grown fare. Horse-riding excursions can be organised from the farm and overnight accommodation is available.

The Roman outpost of Volubilis

Roman town of ★★ **Volubilis** (open daily 8.30am–5 or 6pm; if you get a taxi from Moulay Idriss, it is a good idea to ask your driver to wait if you don't want to walk back). As the capital of the African province of Mauritania Tingitana, Volubilis flourished both economically and culturally from AD42–285. At the beginning of its history, it had an unusually long period of peace, which made a defensive wall unnecessary.

The ruins demonstrate how prosperous the inhabitants were; the 50 olive presses that were found show that olive oil was a prime source of their wealth.

A TOUR OF THE SITE

Individual buildings are clearly labelled; from the entrance to the site, follow the footpath through the olive grove and over the Fertassa river, and proceed in a clockwise direction to reach the House of Orpheus (mosaic in situ) and the Baths of Gallienus (on the left), and a little further on the Capitol and Basilica on the right. From the fine Triumphal Arch, built by Marcus Aurelius Sebastenus in honour of Caracalla, the Decumanus Maximus leads northeast to the Tangier Gate.

The street is flanked by the remains of many fine villas, some of which are named after the mosaics they contain. Look out for the Acrobat's House and the House of Venus (with lovely mosaics depicting the abduction of Hylas by nymphs and the bathing Diana being surprised by Acteon). The villas were also the source of several superb bronzes now on display in Rabat's Archaeological Museum *(see page 26)*. The House of Ephebus, for example, yielded a beautiful statue of an *ephebe* (young man), and the House of Nereids contained the bronze heads of Cato and Juba II; both villas contain fine mosaics.

It was only when the attacks by the Berbers became more frequent that a wall with 10 gates was built round Volubilis. The **Tangier Gate** still stands on the northern edge of the site. The city went into decline and the Romans retreated to Tingis, present-day Tangier.

4: Fes

A visit to the city of Fes (pop. 770,000) is one of the highlights of any tour of Morocco. In its old city of Fes el-Bali it is as if nothing has changed since the Middle Ages. Enclosed within its walls, the city appears timeless, an interlocking structure of mosques, *madrassas*, palaces, *fondouks* (inns for merchants) and souks in which traditional trades still thrive. At its heart is the Karouyine Mosque, a centre of Islamic learning since the 9th century. To this day Fes is considered the intellectual capital of Morocco and one of the most important cultural cities in the Maghreb.

Map on page 43

Star Attraction
● Volubilis

Below: a shrewd Fassi
Bottom: Bab Bou Jeloud

HISTORY

Fes is the cradle of the Moroccan monarchy. Its first representative was Moulay Idriss I, a political refugee and a great-grandson of the Prophet's daughter Fatima. After an unsuccessful uprising against the caliphate in Baghdad, he fled in 786 from his home in Medina to Volubilis *(see page 40)*, where the local Berber tribes embraced Islam and appointed him *imam* (holy leader) in 788.

Idriss I accelerated the spread of Islam and the Arab influence in the Maghreb. He assembled his followers by the Oued Fes in a camp by the name of Madinat Fas. In 793, two months after his

Map on page 43

Below: souk trader
Bottom: Fes el-Bali

death, his son was born to his Berber concubine Kenza. At the age of 11, the child, Moulay Idriss II (804–828), was appointed *imam*. Later, he transformed the Berber camp of his father into an Arabian capital.

In the 9th century, educated Arabs exiled from Kairouan in Tunisia, and skilled Muslim and Jewish craftsmen expelled from Córdoba, contributed to the city's rapid rise to prosperity. With the building of the Karouyine Mosque in 859, a tradition of Koranic scholarship was begun which is still greatly respected in the Islamic world.

Fes reached its cultural high point in the 13th and 14th centuries as the capital of the Merinid dynasty. The oldest of the four imperial cities, it was the political, economic and cultural centre of the country. When the French transferred their centre of power to Rabat and Casablanca, Fes remained the spiritual and religious capital.

CITY TOUR

Like all the older Moroccan cities, Fes consists of a walled medina and a new town – Ville Nouvelle – laid out by the colonialists, but in the case of Fes the old town is in turn divided into Fes el-Bali, founded in 800 by the Idrissids, and the later Fes el-Jdid ('Fes the New'), built by the Merinids in the 13th century.

The attractive Ville Nouvelle is bisected by the wide, palm-lined Avenue Hassan II. Place Mohammed V is dominated by three corner cafés – La Renaissance, Le Cristal and La Koutoubia – which are pleasant places in which to pass the time and watch the passing scene. The tourist office is also on the square.

AN OVERVIEW

To get an idea of the geography of Fes, it is worth making a circuit by taxi of the hills surrounding the city. Follow the Boulevard Allal el-Fassi and the turning up to the **Borj Sud ❶**, a fortress built in the 16th century by the Saadian Ahmed el-Mansour. The jumble of houses spreading up the hill above the river valley is Fes el-Bali. The horizon is dominated by the 902-m (2,959-ft) Jbel Zalagh. Another good view of the three city districts can be obtained from the **Merinid tombs** ❷, on the hill behind the Palais Jamai Hotel near Bab Jamai. The tombs contain the remains of the last Merinid sultans. There is a no less attractive view from **Borj Nord** ❸, the counterpart of Borj Sud, close to the Hotel Merinides (whose bar terrace offers lovely evening views). The fortress doubles as an arms museum (erratic opening times).

FES EL-JDID

The starting point for a tour of the medina of ★★ **Fes el-Jdid** is the **Royal Palace** ❹. This huge palace complex (not open to the public) was begun by the Merinids and has been continuously enlarged ever since. Behind the gilt bronze doors of the monumental gate, built in 1969–71, are extensive palaces, gardens, parade squares, a Merinid *madrassa* and a mosque.

    ★★★ **Fes el-Bali** is entered through the **Bab Bou Jeloud** ❺. This tripled-arched gate, dating from

Star Attractions
- ● **Fes el-Jdid**
- ● **Fes el-Bali**

The Mellah
Tucked into the southeastern corner of Fes el-Jdid is the Jewish quarter or *mellah* ('salt'), a term believed to allude to the Jews' job of draining and salting the heads of decapitated rebels before they were impaled on the gates of the town. The once thriving Jewish community has dwindled considerably. The Hebrew Cemetery (7am–sunset, closed Sat) lies on the edge of the quarter, near the Place des Alaouites.

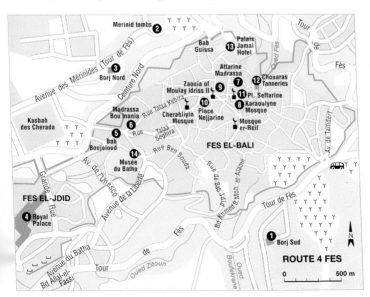

ROUTE 4 FES

only 1913, was built in the traditional Moorish style. The outer side is decorated with blue-glazed tiles, while the side facing the medina has green faïence arabesques.

THE BOU INANIA MADRASSA

Picturesquely framed in the archway of Bab Bou Jeloud are two minarets, the smaller one belonging to the Mosque of Sidi-Lazzaz, the larger one to the ★★**Madrassa Bou Inania** ❻ (open daily 9am–noon, 2.30–5 or 6pm; closed Fri until 3pm), one of the country's few buildings in religious use that can be entered by non-Muslims. Built by Sultan Abou Inan between 1351–58, it was intended to be the largest and most splendid Islamic college in Fes. The entrance, off Talaa Kebira, gives no hint of the elaborately decorated interior, which is a splendid showcase of Merinid craftwork. The quality of the cedarwood carving, stucco work and *zellige* work (mosaic tiling) is outstanding, testifying to the aesthetic leanings of the ruler who built the *madrassa*. The most lavish decoration is found in the *mihrab* (niche) in the prayer hall.

Opposite the *madrassa* is the **Bou Inania water-clock**. This 14th-century clock, constructed at the behest of Abou Inan to ring out the hours of prayer, has been silent for five centuries. Restoration work, commissioned by UNESCO

Below and bottom: roofs and courtyard of the Karouyine Mosque

some years ago, has so far failed to make the 13 little bronze hammers strike the same number of bronze bowls and accurately mark time.

TALAA KEBIRA

There is a bewildering contrast between the meditative stillness of the *madrassa* and the noisy **Talaa Kebira** ('Big Hill') descending into the labyrinth of Fes el-Bali. Hammering and banging resounds from the many little workshops; loaded donkeys steer a path through the crowds accompanied by the drovers' cries of '*Balak balak*', warning people to move out of the way.

Near the Karouyine Mosque are the souks selling luxury goods, such as fine fabrics, perfumes and slippers. Near the **Souk Attarine** (perfume souk) is another splendid example of Merinid art, the ★★**Attarine Madrassa** ❼ (open 9am–1pm and 3–6.30pm) built by Sultan Abou Said in 1322. Like the Bou Inania, it has an inner courtyard of great elegance. As the *madrassa* is no longer in use, you can enter the prayer hall and gain access to the roof (tip the custodian) for views over the green roofs and the blue and white tiled courtyard of the Karouyine Mosque.

KAROUYINE MOSQUE

The ★★**Karouyine Mosque** ❽ (closed to non-Muslims) is the centrepiece of the medina. Founded in 859 by Lalla Fatima al-Fihrya, a pious woman from Kairouan in Tunisia who wished to build a small prayer hall in memory of her father, the mosque has expanded over the centuries into the second largest mosque in Morocco and one of the most splendid in the world.

It was enlarged and embellished under the Almohads and Merinids (the latter also added the library, containing a unique collection of illuminated Koranic manuscripts, off Place Seffarine). In the 16th century, the Saadians added two fountain pavilions in Andalusian style to the courtyard.

The 16-aisled prayer hall is supported by 270 pillars made of marble and porphyry. Non-

Star Attractions
- Attarine Madrassa
- Karouyine Mosque

Beauty bazaar
Just off Souk Attarine is Souk el-Henna, selling all manner of traditional cosmetics and toiletries. You will find baskets of green henna leaves (which are boiled to make a paste to colour hair and decorate the hands and feet); antimony to line the eyes; rose water, white clay and argan oil for the complexion; black soap for cleansing the body; and a red cream made from poppy powder and the bark of the pomegranate tree to colour the lips.

View over Fes el-Bali

Map on page 43

Muslims can only gain an impression of all this splendour by peering through one of the 14 bronze doors that open onto the mosque.

ZAOUIA OF MOULAY IDRISS II

To the west of the mosque is the ★★ **Zaouia of Moulay Idriss II** ❾, the mausoleum of the founder of Fes. A popular place of pilgrimage, it is flanked by tiny shops selling nougat, dates, nuts, and a large selection of votive candles. The mausoleum acquired its present form between the 18th and 19th centuries; non-Muslims can glimpse the antechamber through the open doors.

The ★★ **Place Nejjarine** ❿ (wood-working souk) is just west of the *zaouia* (follow the scent of cedar wood). The elaborate **Nejjarine Fountain** forming the focal point of the square has been restored, along with the *fondouk* (inn for merchants), which has been turned into an excellent **museum** (10am–7pm) of wood-working techniques and tools. The museum's stylish roof-top café offers cooling drinks, mint tea and views.

PLACE SEFFARINE AND THE TANNERIES

On the east side of the Karouyine Mosque, next to the Koranic Library, is **Place Seffarine** ⓫, a picturesque square devoted to metalworkers. From

Below and bottom: Exterior detail and interior of the Zaouia of Moulay Idriss II

here it is a short walk north to the ★★**Chouaras Tanneries** (closed Fri), one of Fes's most memorable sights – and indeed smells. The methods used here have not changed for centuries. The hides are first washed, cured and cleaned of any residue flesh, soaked in urine to make them supple and then dyed in open-air vats. To get the best views of the paintbox network of pits where the skins are soaked and dyed, climb up to the terrace of one of the shops that have sprung up around the dyers.

Further north the route leads to the luxurious **Palais Jamai Hotel** beside Bab Jamai. Built at the end of the 19th century as a palace for the viziers of Sultan Moulay Hassan, the hotel is a great place to stay, dine or have tea in the gardens.

BATHA MUSEUM

If you have time during your visit to Fes, it is worthwhile visiting the ★**Musée Du Batha** (Place de l'Istiqlal; open 9am–noon, 2.30–5.30pm; closed Tues), in the 19th-century palace of a vizier. Its magnificently carved and painted double doors open onto a garden courtyard laid with mosaics. Among the displays, illustrated Korans, ceramics, carved furniture, woven articles, embroidery, carpets and domestic utensils all help to flesh out traditional life in Fes.

EXCURSION TO MOULAY YACOUB

The hills around Fes and Meknes are known for their springs, which in many cases are linked to *marabout* (tombs of holy men) and are thus popular pilgrimage sites. Of those near Fes, **Moulay Yacoub**, 20km (12 miles) north of the city makes a pleasant excursion; buses to the village leave from the station near Borj Nord.

The focal point of the spa is the **Marabout of Moulay Yacoub**, above the miracle-working hot sulphur spring. In 1989, below the original village built on terraces, a new spa was opened to treat rheumatism and ear, nose and throat disorders. Here, belief in miracles and orthodox medicine go hand in hand.

Star Attractions
• Zaouia of Moulay Idriss II
• Place Nejjarine

Luxurious slippers
Fes is famous for its pointed slippers called *babouches*. Sewn by hand, they are made from three types of leather: soft goatskin linings, calf-leather uppers and thick leather soles (from the head of the animal). Expect to pay 150 Dh for the best quality *babouches*. The classic colour for men's *babouches* is yellow. Women's babouches are often decorated with gold thread.

Leather-workers dip hides in Chouaras Tanneries

Map on page 50

Evening assembly
The piazza and garden beneath the Koutoubia make a popular early evening focus for *Marrakshis* and visitors alike. The assembled families create an enjoyable atmosphere in which to stroll and admire the mosque. The terrace café of Hotel Islane opposite the mosque offers a good view of the mosque and the evening scene.

5: Marrakech

In summer, a paralysing heat broods over the city of Marrakech; in winter, the snowy peaks of the High Atlas glitter from afar. The massive, clay-coloured defensive wall of the medina contrasts with the wide boulevards and open plan of the Ville Nouvelle (known as Gueliz).

Marrakech (pop. 745,000) is one of the great cities of Africa. Ruck-sack loaded globetrotters fall in love with it, as do the rich and famous. Whether one is staying in a luxury hotel such as La Mamounia or in an exclusive villa in the *palmerie*, or are obliged to make do with one of the basic hotels, Marrakech fulfils everyone's idea of an oriental fantasy.

HISTORY

Shortly after coming to power in 1062, the Almoravides established a camp at this strategically important location just to the north of the Atlas Mountains. This rapidly expanded to become the capital of the Almoravide realm, and by 1126 it was surrounded by a defensive wall. From 1147, the city prospered under the Almohads, who added the Koutoubia mosque, the lovely minaret of which is a useful orientation point in the city to this day. In the 13th century, the

Street performers on the Jemaa el-Fna

ruling Merinids transferred the capital to Fes. Their successors, the Saadians, moved it back to Marrakech in the 16th century, when the flourishing caravan trade with sub-Saharan Africa and the export of raw sugar ushered in an era of unprecedented prosperity. At this time, Moulay Ahmed el-Mansour ad-Dahbi built El Badi Palace.

From 1912, the Haouz Plain was settled by French colonists, and the finest colonial city in the Maghreb was created outside the walled medina. Trade, agriculture and tourism still guarantee a balanced economic structure. The town is also the seat of the university of Cadi Ayad.

CITY TOUR

For 800 years, the 77-m (252-ft) minaret of the **★★Koutoubia Mosque** ('Mosque of the Booksellers'; closed to non-Muslims) ❶, built by the Almohads, has been the symbol of the city. The 3-km (2-mile) long Avenue Mohammed V, lined with orange trees, would be unthinkable without its ochre-coloured minaret, with its elegant tracery and diamond reliefs. The minaret served as a model for the Tour Hassan in Rabat and the Giralda in Seville. Next to the tower is a *koubba* (tomb) for Lalla Zohra Bint el-Kouch, daughter of a prince from black Africa who lived in the 17th century and is revered as a saint.

THE SAADIAN TOMBS

South of the mosque, close to Bab Agnaou, are the **★★Saadian Tombs** ❷ (Tombeaux Saadian; daily 8.30am–noon, 2.30–6pm), built in the second half of the 16th century by Sultan Moulay Ahmed el-Mansour ad-Dahbi (known as 'the Golden'). They contain the tombs of 62 members of the Saadian dynasty. The complex was only rediscovered in 1917, having been bricked up by the Alaouite Moulay Ismail in the 17th century.

The complex is divided into chambers. The Hall of the Twelve Columns is rated as the finest architectural work of this epoch. On the walls of the mausoleum, polychrome tile mosaics, stucco

Star Attractions
● Koutoubia Mosque
● Saadian Tombs

Below: hawker in the souk
Bottom: Saadian Tombs

Map below

work inscription friezes and arabesques are masterfully blended to form a filigree decor of great beauty. Beneath the dome of carved and gilded cedarwood, supported by 12 white pillars of Carrara marble, are the three sarcophagi of Sultan Ahmed el-Mansour, his son and successor and his grandson.

In the smaller mausoleum is the tomb of Lalla Messaouda, mother of El Mansour, with numerous ladies of the court buried close by. Evidence of the high infant mortality rate of the times is found in the many small graves.

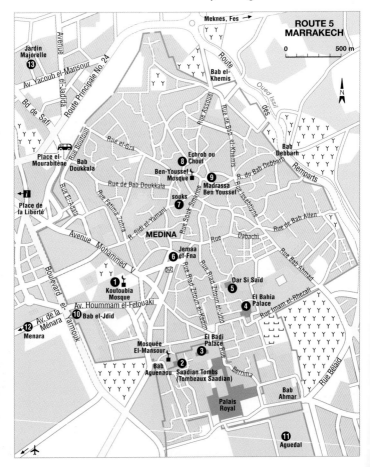

PALACES

The remains of ★ **El Badi Palace ❸** (open daily 8.30–11.45am and 2.30–5.45pm) bear witness to the wealth accumulated by the Saadian Sultan Moulay Ahmed el-Mansour through the gold and slave trades. Sixteenth-century chroniclers described 360 rooms, each one expensively designed with Carrara marble, onyx, faïence mosaics, stucco work and carved ceilings covered in gold leaf. However, this splendid creation of the most powerful of the Saadians was demolished a century later by the Alaouite Sultan Moulay Ismail, who plundered its stone for his own palaces in Meknes.

An idea of the lifestyle of a grand vizier at the end of the 19th century is provided by ★ **El Bahia Palace ❹** (open 9am–noon, 3–6pm). Covering an area of 6 hectares (15 acres), it has 150 rooms with double doors opening onto gardens, fragrant with jasmine and citrus fruits, and marble-tiled inner courtyards gleaming in the sun. The luxury of an oriental court is reflected in the reception and private rooms. Bahia ('the brilliant'), the woman who gave her name to the palace, bore the grand vizier Ba Ahmed a son, as the first of his four wives.

MUSEUM

A short walk from El Bahia Palace is the ★ **Dar Si Saïd ❺** (daily 9am–noon and 3–6pm; closed Tues), which is worth seeing not only for its excellent collection of regional arts and crafts. The palace, which was built in 1895 at the same time as El Bahia Palace, was the home of the grand vizier Ba Ahmed's brother, Si Saïd, a chamberlain and vizier of Hassan I. The richly carved and colourfully painted ceilings and double doors of these rooms are fine examples of the sophisticated wood-carving of this period.

On display are Berber jewellery, costumes, cases of weaponry, examples of copper, silver and brassware, and on the second floor an interesting collection of antique carpets which are particularly worth seeking out if you intend to buy a carpet in Morocco and want to get an idea of quality.

June festival
In June an international folk festival is held in the ruins of El Badi, featuring troupes from many Arab countries. In addition to the concerts and performances, a *fantasia* takes place at 5pm each evening. A well-loved element of most large festivals in Morocco, *fantasias* involve charging horsemen performing daring manoeuvres and acrobatics to the accompaniment of gunfire.

Below: view from Madrassa Ben Youssef
Bottom: El Badi Palace ruins

Map on page 50

Below and bottom: the dyers' quarter

JEMAA EL-FNA

On the central square of ★★★ **Jemaa el-Fna** ('Meeting place of the Dead') ❻, the heads of those who had been executed used to be mounted on long spears and put on display. Today, in the late afternoon, it is the travelling performers who attract the attention of both tourists and local people. Although the look of the place has changed since the wooden stalls were torn down in the 1980s, the show goes on. In 1994, the Jemaa el-Fna was given another face-lift and now has neat lines of drinks stalls. In the evening the mobile kitchens move in, each providing an astonishing array of snacks cooked on the spot and eaten at adjoining tables. The menus include sheep's heads, snails in a cumin-flavoured liquor, *merguez* (spicy sausages) and *harira* (a thick broth). Entertainment is provided by snake charmers, story-tellers, acrobats and whirling Gnaoua dancers.

THE SOUKS

The ★★★ **souks** ❼ of Marrakech are the most extensive in Morocco. Spreading north from the Jemaa el-Fna, off Rue Semmarine, and divided according to craft, the workshops and shops of the potters, wool-dyers, metal-workers and wood-turners are open to the eyes of passers-by.

In the dyers' quarter, bundles of brightly dyed wool hang from the house walls; the Kissaria, devoted to luxury goods, is hung with shimmering kaftans and glittering ladies' *babouches* (slippers) cover the walls; in the copper bazaar, beautifully shaped vessels wink in the sunlight. Between the shops, arched doorways under carved canopies lead into *hammams*, old *fondouks* (inns) or mosques. Every quarter has a wall fountain; an inscription on the monumental fountain **Echrob ou Chouf** ❽ exhorts passers-by to 'drink and admire'.

PLACE BEN YOUSSEF

North of the souks, on Place Ben Youssef, the ★★ **Madrassa Ben Youssef** ❾ (open daily 9am–noon, 3–6pm; but may be closed for restoration) was founded by the Merinid Abou el-Hassan in the 14th century, and developed by the Saadians as the largest Koran school in the Maghreb. Double doors embellished with bronze reliefs lead into a courtyard tiled in Carrera marble with a pool at the centre. An octagonal carved dome arches over the prayer hall, dimly lit by small arched windows with pierced filigree stucco work.

Next to the *madrassa* is the **Ben Youssef Mosque** (closed to non-Muslims), rebuilt in the 19th century, and in the impressively restored Menehbi Palace the privately-funded ★ **Musée de Marrakech** (9am–12.30pm and 3–6.30pm, closed Mon), which displays an eclectic collection of antiques and rare manuscripts and hosts contemporary exhibitions and concerts. The splendid palace itself is well worth seeing; its courtyard has an excellent bookshop and café.

THE GATES

Between 6–9m (20–30ft) high, and fortified by approximately 200 bastions, the city wall of packed clay is a massive construction. The best way to appreciate it is to take a trip around the perimeter *(tour des remparts)* in a *calèche* (a horse-drawn cab); fares are posted inside the cabs, though you should expect to pay more. The 13-km (8-mile) tour takes in 10 differently constructed gates,

Star Attractions
● **Jemaa el-Fna**
● **the souks**
● **Madrassa Ben Youssef**

Architectural first
The oldest and possibly the most significant monument in Marrakech is the often overlooked Almoravide Cupola dating from the beginning of the 12th century, situated next to the Musée de Marrakech. It is the only surviving pure Almoravide building in Morocco and is thus a unique monument to the dynasty that first united the country into a single kingdom. Its elegant underside was the precursor of the stalactite plaster decoration that became the hallmark of Moorish architectural decoration and culminated in the Alhambra Palace in Granada.

The Jemaa el-Fna

Map on page 50

Picture perfect
If you want to see the snow-covered Atlas rising over the pavilion and pool of the Menara, a view captured on countless postcards, you must time your visit for sunset during the first few months of the year.

Below: the Menara pavilion
Bottom: Jardin Majorelle

starting at the **Bab el-Jdid** ❿. The **Bab Aguenaou**, with its rich stone relief decoration, is especially worth a stop, as are the **Bab Ahmar**, a vaulted passage 17m (56ft) deep, the **Bab Debbarh**, built by the Almoravides, and the 21m (69ft) deep **Bab el-Khemis**. The gatehouse of **Bab Doukkala**, just west of the dyers' quarter, has been converted into a gallery showing works by local and international artists.

GARDENS OF DELIGHT

Marrakech is a garden city. As well as its extensive *palmerie* (sandwiched between the Fes and and Casablanca roads), it has several famous gardens that make inviting escapes from the heat and dust of the medina and new town. The best way to visit them is by *calèche* during the late afternoon, when the heat has died down.

Aguedal ⓫ (open daily 8.30am–6pm), south of the royal palace, is based on the extensive agricultural estate laid out in the 12th century by the Almohads, and walled by Hassan I in the 19th century. More popular with visitors, however, are the ★ **Menara** gardens ⓬ (open 8.30am–6pm), 2.5-km (1½-mile) west of Bab el-Jdid, with their romantic pavilion and pool, which on a clear day are outlined against a backdrop of the High Atlas.

Off the road to Fes, north of the medina, is the ★ **Jardin Majorelle** ⓭ (Avenue Moulay Yaacoub el-Mansour; open daily 8am–noon, 2–6pm), planted by the orientalist painter Jacques Majorelle (1886–1962), who lived in the villa here in the 1920s. The garden is based on the botanical souvenirs collected on Majorelle's many journeys through Africa, from the Atlas to the Ivory Coast. With the many different greens of the plants set in azure tubs, together with pools and waterfalls, Majorelle created a uniquely beautiful work of art. Delicate bamboo plants and islands of cacti contrast with the bright colours of the flowers, reflecting the compositional skills of the artist.

The property was restored some time ago by the fashion designer Yves Saint-Laurent, who is a part-time resident of Marrakech.

Excursion to the Atlas

OURIKA–OUKAIMEDEN

When seen on a clear winter's day from the ramparts of Marrakech, the snow-capped Atlas Mountains seem almost close enough to reach out and touch. In reality, their northern flanks are about an hour's drive away by car and a little longer by bus (buses leave Marrakech from Bab er Rob, near the Royal Palace).

Below: Ourika Valley
Bottom: valley life

The most popular short excursion is to the Ourika Valley (Vallée d'Ourika), beyond the village of Arhbalou (1,025m/3,363ft) on the S513 southeast of Marrakech. Follow the valley to the village of **Setti-Fatma**, 24km (15 miles) from Marrakech, at a height of 1,500m (4,921ft). As the starting point of trekking tours, the village has a number of inns and restaurants. In summer *Marrakshis* and young tourists come to swim in a series of seven waterfalls on the far side of the river.

West of Arhbalou, a road leads to **Oukaïmeden** (72km/45 miles), one of the main bases for skiing. The plateau, at a height of 2,650m (8,694ft) on the Jbel Oukaïmeden (3,273m/10,738ft), has hotels and lifts. From here, serious hikers can make the descent to **Asni** (1,150m/3,773ft), a springboard for exploring the Toubkal National Park *(see page 71)* and one of the large villages on the Tizi-n-Test pass.

Map on page 57

6: Tangier

'I feel at the moment like a dreamer gazing at things which he fears will vanish before his eyes,' wrote the painter Eugène Delacroix during his stay in Tangier in 1832. The special atmosphere of this harbour town (pop. 526,000) is derived from its unique geography and its mixture of Arab and European influences. The Straits of Gibraltar connect not only Europe and Africa, but also the Mediterranean and the Atlantic.

Tangier also has the hint of disrepute common to many ports, permeated by the melancholy of past glory.

HISTORY

The city's position at the mouth of the Mediterranean has made it an important port since ancient times. The Carthaginian seafarer Hanno anchored off Tangier, then called Tingis, in 5BC; under the Romans it shipped grain from North Africa to Rome. With the advance of the Muslim Arabs a new era began. The city fell successively to the Almoravides, the Almohads and the Merinids, and in 1471 it was captured by the Portuguese. Through the marriage of Charles II to Catherine of Braganza, the city came under English domination in 1661, but the Alaouite Moulay Ismail forced the invaders to retreat in 1684.

In the late 19th and early 20th centuries, the strategically desirable port was an object of dispute amongst the European colonial powers. When it was declared an international zone in 1923, a fever of trading activity ensued and the new town expanded rapidly. When this special status ended in 1956, the fortunes of the city began to decline, and only smugglers and hash dealers valued its proximity to the Spanish exclave of Ceuta along the coast.

But the future is looking brighter. The city is expanding rapidly, and although European tourism is not as healthy as it used to be, the city remains a favourite summer destination for holidaying Moroccans. An important new development, the

Writers and artists

Tangier has long been a magnet for western artists and writers. As early as 1832, the Orientalist painter Eugène Delacroix said of the city, 'At every step, one meets ready-made paintings that would bring 20 generations of painters wealth and glory.' Later, Matisse made two fruitful visits to the city in 1912 and 1913, painting the views from his room in Hôtel Villa de France, and in the 1950s Francis Bacon spent three years in Tangier. The city also drew many writers, including William Burroughs, who wrote episodes of *The Naked Lunch* in his room in Hotel Muniria (Rue Magellan), and Paul Bowles, who lived here from the 1950s until his death in 1999 and was constantly inspired by Moroccan themes.

Tangier, gateway to Africa

creation of a new duty-free port south of the city,
is set to boost economic prosperity further.

CITY TOUR

Tangier's relatively small medina clusters above
the old port, while the new town spreads east
and south. To the west is the district of Montagne,
a villa suburb in which palaces belonging to the
Moroccan and Saudi-Arabian royal families nes-
tle among pine trees.

Most of Tangier's historic sites are in the medina, but the new town offers good cafés and bars,
some attractive colonial architecture, the elegant
El Minzah hotel and the beach. Its central spine
is **Avenue Pasteur** (tourist office and main
banks), off which run the main streets for shops
and restaurants. At **Place de France**, Rue de la
Liberté leads downhill to the **Grand Socco ❶**,
and the keyhole-shaped gate to the ★ **medina**. On
the west side of the square, you can just see the

Tangier's excellent beach

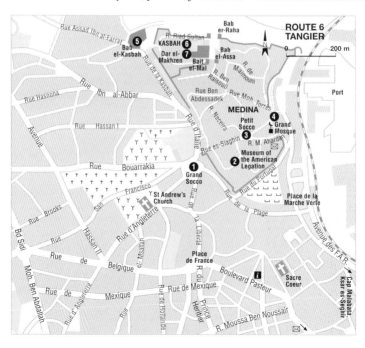

Map on page 57

English influence

The British Anglican Church of St Andrew's, just off the Grand Socco, was built in 1894 on land given by Sultan Moulay Hassan. The church serves mainly Tangier's Anglophone expat community, some of whom have lived in Tangier for four generations. Mustapha, the church's caretaker, is more than happy to take visitors on a tour of the graveyard and to point out details of the Moorish influenced interior, including the Lord's Prayer written in Arabic on the chancel arch.

Clothed in carpets, Tangier

minaret of the Mosque of Sidi-Bouabid with its coloured tiles; this was the first mosque to be built outside the medina.

From the keyhole arch, **Rue es-Siaghin** ('Street of the Silversmiths'), a busy shopping street, cuts into the medina. A right turn along here leads to the ★ **Museum of the American Legation ❷** (8, Zankat America; open 9am–12.30pm, 3–6.30pm; closed Tues), documenting the diplomatic relationships between Morocco and the United States. Exhibits in the elegant 19th-century building include the correspondence between George Washington and Sultan Moulay Abdallah.

Rue es-Siaghin leads to the **Petit Socco ❸**, the heart of the medina. In the 1920s, this area was a red-light district, and its cafés still have a slight air of disrepute. Just beyond here is the **Grand Mosque ❹**, which Moulay Ismail built on the original site of a Roman temple

THE KASBAH

In the northwestern corner of the old city wall, the **Bab el-Kasbah ❺** opens onto the **Kasbah ❻**, the highest part of the medina. Inside, the narrow Rue Riad Sultan runs along the northern part of the wall. The best panoramic view is from the restaurant Le Détroit. There is also a good view of the Straits from the Bab er-Raha in the north wall.

On the Place de la Kasbah, a Moorish gate framed in glazed tiles leads into the museum of the ★ **Dar el-Makhzen** ❼ (open summer 9am–noon and 3–6pm; winter 9am–3.30pm; closed Tues), a palace built by Moulay Ismail in the 17th century. The ground floor rooms display arts and crafts and the upper floor has a collection of antiquities with copies of the important Hellenistic bronze sculptures from Volubilis *(see page 40)*. In the entrance hall of the museum is the Bait el-Mal treasury.

The Bab el-Assa, where floggings took place, leads out of the kasbah. Follow the busy alleys of the souks down into the centre of the medina to reach the Petit Socco.

Excursions

CAP MALABATA – KSAR ES-SEGHIR

The coast road east of Tangier passes several small beaches and on clear days offers good views across the Straits to Spain. **Cap Malabata** (11km/7 miles) has a lighthouse and a small café. At **Ksar es-Seghir** (33km/20 miles east of Tangier), several cafés and a fish restaurant offer views over a pretty Portuguese fort built on the mouth of a small river.

Below: Cap Spartel lighthouse
Bottom: the Caves of Hercules

CAP SPARTEL

At **Cap Spartel** (14km/9 miles west of Tangier), another lighthouse marks the spot where the Mediterranean meets the Atlantic. Sunsets from the cape are often spectacular, and can be watched from the terrace of the fish restaurant Mirage or from one of the makeshift cafés that spring up above the rocky bays in summer.

The **Caves of Hercules** (9am–sunset), 4km (2½ miles) further south, were inhabited in pre-historic times. One kilometre (½ mile) further on are the sparse ruins of the Roman trading centre of **Cotta**, dating from the 2nd and 3rd centuries. So far, a bath house and the remains of a temple have been excavated.

Map
on page
62

7: On the Portuguese Trail

Agadir – Essaouira – Safi – El Jadida – Casablanca (540km/336 miles)

The string of fortified ports along the Atlantic coast is a legacy of the Portuguese, who between the 15th and 17th centuries captured several of Morocco's coastal towns.

The rocky coastline is interspersed with wide sandy beaches, dotted with brightly-coloured tents in summer, when families come to camp here, sometimes for weeks at a time. The hinterland north of Essaouira is generally flat, with narrow terraces chequered with vegetable plots or salt pans on the coastal side of the road, and undulating green or golden cornfields on the landward side. Small farmers and large-scale agricultural businesses exist side by side, and in late summer/early autumn you are just as likely to see huge combine harvesters as open-air threshing floors with donkeys plodding round them.

The gnarled argan trees particular to southwest Morocco dominate as far north as Safi. Amidst the thick branches goats demonstrate their tree-climbing skills, willing to risk their necks to get at the luscious green fruit.

If you stop to visit the beaches and fortified towns, this journey will take about four days by car, staying overnight in Essaouira, Safi and El Jadida. You may want to linger longer; Essaouira, in particular, is a great place to relax, with good restaurants and accommodation, a laid-back atmosphere and a sandy beach plus rock pools for children.

Below: relic of Essaouira's turbulent past
Bottom: Agadir's beach

AGADIR

Agadir (pop.185,000) was reconstructed after the devastating earthquake of 1960, and has no special atmosphere, let alone a recognisable centre. By way of compensation there are 8km (5 miles) of sandy beach, good sports, restaurants and entertainment facilities and a wide variety of hotels.

If you want to see something more authentically Moroccan, there are many worthwhile excursions from the city *(see page 65)*. In Agadir itself, the fishing and trade port can be visited and the weekend market is popular. The hill on which the kasbah stood before the earthquake has a panoramic view of the city and bay.

NORTH OF AGADIR

The first stage of this route runs close to the coast. North of Agadir, a series of inviting sandy beaches offer more privacy than the city beach. At **Tamri**, 56km (35 miles) from Agadir, the centre of banana production, the road veers away from the sea to pass through gently rolling hills planted with argan trees. Shortly after Tamanar, a side road curves down to **Cap Tafelney**, the site of a fish-processing plant. The road then climbs for 7km (4.3 miles) in the direction of Jbel Amsittene (905m /2,969ft), from where there is a good view of the surrounding countryside.

> **Music of the Gnaoua**
> The Essaouira Gnaoua festival, inaugurated in 1998, celebrates Morocco's tribal soul music. It has quickly become a huge international music festival with musicians from all over the world. Usually held in June, it is the largest annual free music festival in Morocco.
>   For details, contact the website: www.festival-gnaoua.co.ma

ESSAOUIRA

The dunes just outside ★★★ **Essaouira** (pop. 56,000), 173km/107 miles from Agadir, are protected from the wind by acacias and junipers. Though developed as a trading port by the Arabs and fortified by the Portuguese, the town you see today was built in the 1760s by Sultan Sidi Mohammed to replace Agadir as Marrakech's

Fortified Essaouira

ROUTE 7

0   50 km

Casablanca
Rabat
Dar-Bouâzza
Aïn-ej-Jmel
Bir-Jdid
Tnine-des-Chtouka
Azemmour
El Jadida
Moulay-Abdallah
Port de Jorf-Lasfar
Oued Oum er Rbia
Boulâouane
Sidi-Moussa
Sidi-Smaïl
Sidi-Bennour
Oualidia
Khemis-des-Zemamra
Cap Beddouza
Youssoufia
Safi
Bouguedra
Sebt-des-Gzoula
Tnine-Rhiate
Oued Tensift
Talmest
Chichaoua
Marrakech
Sidi-Moktar
Ounara
Imi-n-Tanoute
Essaouira
Smimou
Jbel Amsittene 905
Cap Tafelney
Tamanar
Tamri
Oued Sous
Taghazoute
Oulad-Teïma
Agadir
Aït-Melloul
Inezgane

chief port. Formerly known as Mogador, a corruption of a Berber word for 'safe anchorage', it perches on a rocky peninsula surrounded by fortifications, a legacy of the Portuguese occupation in the 16th century. The unique architecture of the old town, with its straight roads and numerous arched passages, was the work of the French engineer Théodore Cornut.

The Porte de la Marine opens out onto the busy harbour, where, at midday, the appetising aroma of freshly grilled fish served at makeshift stands pervades the air. Immediately behind the Porte de la Marine is the **Skala du Port** – the ramparts – with a battery of 18th-century cannons.

From here there is a view of the town, the harbour and the rocky Isles Purpuraires offshore. Now a bird sanctuary, these islands get their name from the days when a purple dye was extracted from the local shellfish; the Berber king Juba II established a factory to make the dye, which was much in demand in 1st-century Rome. Before this, in the 7th century BC, the islands were a stage post for Phoenician traders on forays down the west coast of Africa. Later on, they were used as a quarantine station for pilgrims returning from Mecca. Boat trips to the islands can be arranged, but you will need permission from the Governor in the province, a formality arranged through the tourist office.

Under the ramparts, a row of carpentry workshops produce crafts and furniture carved from thuja wood, which like the argan is native to the area. To see top-quality inlaid and carved thuja wood, visit the **Musée des Arts et Traditions Populaires Sidi Mohammed Ben Abdallah** in the Rue Laalouj.

In recent years Essaouira has attracted a sizeable community of artists. Some of their work is displayed in the **Galerie d'Art Frederic Damgaard** (Avenue Oqba Ibn Nafiaa, medina).

SAFI, A POTTERS' TOWN

At **Ounara**, 197km (122 miles), dense thuja woods give way to eucalyptus trees and rolling hills. The industrial town of **Safi** (pop. 262,000), 299km (186 miles) is announced by high chimneys and a strong smell of fish. Because of the town's chemical industry and the phosphate harbour, the coastal waters north and south of Safi are not suitable for bathing. The wall enclosing the medina, with its bastions and the ruins of the Dar el-Bahr ('Castle of the Sea'), are reminders of Portuguese rule, though the town reached the height of its prosperity under the Saadian sultans. Today, the fortifications are used during the summer months to stage cultural events.

Safi is proud of a pottery tradition that goes back centuries. Above Bab Chaabah, in the ★ **Quartier de la Ceramique**, smoke rises from the kilns of the largest ceramic centre in Morocco. The **Musée National de la Ceramique**, in the former governor's palace dating from the 18th century, documents the history of Safi ceramics.

The **Marabout of Sidi-Bouzid**, 303km (188 miles), dominates the cliffs north of Safi. The nearby Refuge de Sidi-Bouzid is an inviting restaurant to stop for lunch and a view of the harbour from its terrace. On Cap Beddouza is one of the oldest lighthouses in Morocco, dating from 1915. Beneath it, miles of sandy beach stretch northwards; alongside the road, rows of greenhouses are used for growing tomatoes.

OUALIDIA AND OYSTERS

★ **Oualidia**, 365km (227 miles), is famous for its oyster beds, and the restaurants in the town's two hotels specialise in oysters. It is also a pleasant, low-key resort with good bathing. Many wealthy Moroccans, including the King, have holiday homes in the town.

Moulay Abdallah Amghar is the scene of one of the largest *moussems*, held in August in honour of the holy man of the same name whose mausoleum dominates the village. The festival is attended by falconers in particular.

Map on page 62

Wind-surfing
Signposted off the P8 south of Essaouira is the growing hamlet of Sidi Kaouki, named after a saint buried above its long, sandy beach. Strong winds have made this a favourite spot for wind-surfers and the site of wind-surfing world championships. Small seaside hotels have sprung up away from the beach, offering an alternative base to Essaouira, which can get crowded.

Safi brick-maker

Map
on page
62

Along the sandy beach of **Sidi-Bouzid**, below the domed tomb of the saint, is a concentration of holiday homes. There are also cafés and restaurants, where spiced sardines are a speciality.

EL JADIDA

Below and bottom: a young mother and boys playing, El Jadida

★ **El Jadida** (pop. 120,000), 441km (277 miles), is primarily a seaside town popular with holidaying Moroccans. Its chief sight, a Portuguese cistern, was excavated in 1917, after its discovery under the walled medina that was built in place of the destroyed Portuguese city. The cistern, a columned hall with late-Gothic vaulting, is the town's chief attraction. In the 16th century, it served as a munitions depot before becoming a cistern. A beam of sunlight entering through an opening in the roof and illuminating the room and the vaulting has a magical effect, reflecting in the several inches of water covering the floor.

Azemmour (pop. 32,000), 457km (284 miles), rises above the bank of the Oum er-Rbia river, the largest river in Morocco. In 1486, Portuguese merchants occupied the kasbah, but were expelled in 1541; their cannons now decorate the bastions. The **Bab Mellah** has steps leading up to the battlements, from where there is a view of the medina, the kasbah and the former *mellah*, home to a large Jewish community until the second half of the 20th century. The old town has some splendid houses concealed within its walls.

TO CASABLANCA

The last stretch of the route leads through agricultural areas, past greenhouses and through corn, barley and wheatfields. The route is frequently flanked with produce sellers (strawberries in spring, honeydew melons and cactus fruit in autumn), fishermen selling their catch, and ceramics stalls. Side roads lead down to various beaches along the way.

Eventually, a hazy patch on the horizon indicates **Casablanca**, 540km (336 miles) from Agadir *(see page 29)*.

8: South of Agadir

South of Agadir lie some of the most exhilarating landscapes in Morocco. The dramatic Anti-Atlas mountains crowned by mud villages rise to the southeast; closer to the coast, on the far side of the Oued Massa, about 60km (40 miles) from Agadir, is the start of the Sahara Desert.

Travelling in the region, you will notice Saharan influences in everything from the style of the women's dress to the architecture. Until the 1960s, the Saharan tribes were still leading a nomadic life over an area reaching into black Africa. The spread of modern means of transport, however, forced most of them to settle in one place and pursue sedentary occupations. The few who continue as nomadic livestock breeders still live in tents and sell their sheep and camels in the souks.

Below and bottom: in the camel market, Guelmin

ALONG THE COAST

Leaving Agadir, the road passes through the estuary plains of the Souss. **Inezgane**, 11km (7 miles) south of Agadir, has several hotels but it is primarily a crowded sattelite town and bus junction, with a dreary suburban atmosphere. Just outside the busy trading centre of **Aït-Melloul**, 13km (8 miles), the road crosses the Oued Sous, a river that is vital to the area's rich agriculture.

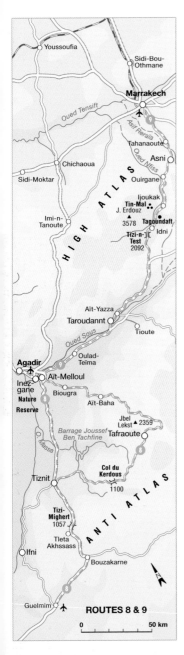

In 1991, the national park of **Sous-Massa** (33,800 hectares/83,520 acres) was created in the coastal area between the estuaries of the Sous and Massa. Its main target is to protect the bald ibis, which is threatened with extinction and breeds only in Morocco. In 1994, addaxes (large antelopes) imported from Germany, Denmark and France, gazelles from Western Sahara and ostriches from Chad were introduced to the park. The reedy wetlands at the estuary of the Massa are home to many marsh and water birds, including pink flamingos.

TIZNIT

On the other side of the Oued Massa is the start of the desert plateau surrounding ★★ **Tiznit** (pop. 43,000), 91km (57 miles). An important trading centre, it originally consisted of 10 separate kasbahs and wasn't enclosed by a 6-km (4-mile) wall until 1882, under Hassan I. When the town expanded further, a new settlement was developed outside the walls.

The main gate, known as the Gate of the Three Windows (marked by the Moroccan Star) leads into the **Méchouar**. Once the parade ground of the French soldiers garrisoned in the town, it is now the lively main square bustling with donkey carts, communal taxis, buses and people. Hotels and cafés are found in the Moorish arcades surrounding the square.

The dominant feature of the medina is the minaret of the **Great Mosque**, dating from the early 20th century. According to tradition, the perches protruding from the tower are the resting place of souls; in reality, they have a more practical function as supports for the painters applying fresh coats of whitewash. North of the mosque is the spring of Lalla Tiznit which, as legend has it, miraculously gushed forth when a pious reformed prostitute, Lalla Tiznit, was martyred. An interesting little souk on Thursdays supplies the population with its everyday needs: vegetables, spices, woven mats, baskets and colourful donkey saddles as well as silver jewellery.

Jewellery from Tiznit is well-known all over Morocco. **Place Kissaria des Bijoutiers** contains shops selling the gold jewellery, often worked in the filigree style favoured in the cities, and traditional silver Berber jewellery. Among the latter are the massive *fibules*, the silver brooches used to pin together a woman's over garment at the shoulders. Common throughout the Berber regions, the *fibule* is often in the form of an inverted triangle with a pin extending at the top that is closed by a circular ring. The most impressive examples come from the Tiznit–Tafraoute region, where they are called *tizerzai*.

TO GUELMIN

South of Tiznit, the road climbs the western ridge of the Anti-Atlas and crosses the Tizi-Mighert, 1,057m (3,468ft) high. From here, when the weather conditions are right, there is a magnificent view over the plateau. Shortly after this, at a height of 1,000m (3,280ft), the road enters **Tleta Akhssass**, which has a Tuesday livestock souk.

Skirting the southern slopes of the western

Map on page 66

Star Attraction
● **Tiznit**

Below: road between Tiznit and Guelmin
Bottom: Tiznit's clay walls

Map on page 66

The real 'blue men'

The blue men are, in theory, the Tuareg of southern Algeria, Mali and Mauritania, whose custom of wearing indigo-dyed headgear stained their faces blue. Sad to say, the true-blue Taureg never ventured as far as Morocco. The only genuine Saharans in Morocco with a claim to being blue are the *Saharoui* from the desert south of Tan Tan, who wear the blue robes of the Mauritanian Kandora. During the Moroccan war against Spanish colonisation of the Western Sahara, and later against the Polisario independence movement, many *Saharoui* refugees migrated into southern Morocco, bringing them into contact with tourists in search of blue men. It was a marketing opportunity not to be missed.

Saharan colours in Guelmin

Anti-Atlas, with its rounded summits and sparse argan forests, the road descends to **Bouzakarne**, 158km (98 miles), at a height of 600m (2,000ft). The reddish-brown stony desert, stunted argan trees, thorny shrubs and grazing flocks of black goats are unmistakeable signs of the encroaching Sahara Desert.

The buildings of **Guelmin** (pop. 73,000), 199km (124 miles), the gate to the Western Sahara, are almost the same colour as the land. The administrative capital of the region, the town is fairly ordinary but friendly, with a basic hotel. While Guelmin has lost its importance as the main base of the caravan trade, its position on the major road from Tangier to Mauritania – the route used for transporting all essential goods into the new towns of the Western Sahara and from the Saharan provinces to Agadir and Casablanca – ensures it remains a busy trading centre and a stopping-point for long-distance lorry drivers.

The Saturday morning livestock market in Guelmin is billed as the camel market of the famous nomadic 'blue men' *(see panel left),* and draws weekly bus tours from Agadir. In reality, just about every carpet dealer and souvenir seller south of the Atlas will attempt to pass himself off as a blue man fresh from the Sahara, so treat any introductions to blue-clad salesmen with a certain amount of sceptism.

DETOUR TO TAFRAOUTE

An alternative route from Agadir to Tiznit involves a detour inland via Tafraoute and the Kerdous Pass (1,110m/3,642ft). This is one of the most exciting routes in Morocco and can be done as part of a round trip from Agadir. It passes first through the barren but impressive rocky landscape of the Anti-Atlas, snaking along the high edge of the mountains, with dramatic views above and below. Cone-shaped outcrops of rock rear out of the valley floor, crowned by agadirs (fortified granaries) and farms. Nothing much grows here, but every so often there are isolated argan trees with goats searching among the branches for the fruits; the occasional cluster of palms and white-domed *koubbas* (tombs of holy men) lift the many shades of pink, ginger and brown.

The high point of the tour is ★★**Tafraoute** (pop. 4,000), superbly located in a high Anti-Atlas valley, 1,000m (3,300ft) above sea level. Erosion has created bizarre natural monuments out of boulders of pink granite, and against this backdrop the residents have also painted their houses pink.

The town centres on a small square, overlooked by the imitation kasbah which is Hotel les Amandiers ('Almonds', an allusion to the almond blossom that decks the area in spring). It is a prosperous town, which benefits from tourism, agriculture and the long-established tradition among the men of seeking their fortune in the cities. Tafraoute businessmen are reputedly among the most successful in Morocco. Sending money home, they build large town-style houses, ready for the day when they retire.

There is not much to see in Tafraoute – the landscape and ambience are the main attractions – but guides will lead you to *Les Roches Bleus*, huge fauvist boulders painted in shades of blue by the Belgian artist Jean Veran, on the edge of town in the direction of Tiznit.

Nearby, in the idyllic valley of the Ammeln tribe, dozens of pink villages cling like birds' nests to the 2,359-m (7,740-ft) Jbel Lekst, below which spread thousands of date palms. These villages are well worth exploring on foot.

Star Attraction
● **Tafraoute**

Below: a resident of Tafraoute
Bottom: Tafraoute town

Map on page 66

9: A Taste of the Atlas

Marrakech – Asni – Tizi-n-Test – Taroudannt – Agadir (304km/189 miles)

The moods and scenery of the Atlas change with the seasons: in the spring, the valleys are full of apple, pear, almond and peach blossom; in the summer, the summits are veiled in mist; in the autumn, brightly attired Berber women can be seen staggering home with bundles of brushwood; and in winter, ice crystals glitter on the branches and smoke rises above the villages.

Below: ammonite for sale
Bottom: Berber village

This trip over the pass of Tizi-n-Test at a height of 2,092m (864ft) is an exhilarating experience in every season. Controlled by the Goundafi tribe until well into the 20th century, the route was once feared by sultans and trading caravans alike. The numerous kasbahs in the high valley of the Nfiss still testify to the former power of the Goundafi.

Overnight stays at Ouirgane and Taroudannt are recommended. The route takes two to three days. Drivers crossing the Tizi-n-Test should take care – the road narrows near the top and the hairpin bends can be treacherous.

LEAVING MARRAKECH

The first section of this route, the stretch from Marrakech *(see page 48)* to Tahanaoute, is bor-

dered by olive groves. Forty percent of the country's olive production comes from more than 8 million olive trees in this region. In the local administrative centre of **Tahanaoute** (34km/21 miles), at a height of 995m (3,264ft), a traditional market is held on Tuesday.

The Saturday souk in **Asni** (1,150m/3,773ft) is the main market for the High Atlas Berbers of the region and has become a regular tourist excursion from Marrakech. The village is splendidly located with impressive views of the nearby summits of the High Atlas. From here it is possible to take a detour to the village of **Imlil**, 17km (10 miles) away (the road deteriorates after 12 km/7 miles, but it is accessible even in a small car). Situated at the foot of ★★ **Mount Toubkal**, the highest peak in North Africa (4,167m/13,670ft), Imlil is the main springboard for hiking expeditions into the Toubkal massif, and from early summer through to autumn it throngs with hikers, mules and mountain guides.

THE NFISS VALLEY

After leaving Asni the road continues to climb. **Ouirgane** has become a popular weekend destination, especially during the hot summer months. At an altitude of about 1,000m (3,300ft), it is considerably cooler than the baking Haouz plain. There is good accommodation in the Roserie, a country-club style hotel (pool, gardens, horse-riding) and in the more modest Sanglier Qui Fume and Chez Momo in the village *(see page 126)*. The village also has a Thursday souk. The road passes through the high **Nfiss Valley**, an area of outstanding beauty studded with clay-walled villages and kasbahs. In summer the area is a particular delight for hikers; the village of **Ijoukak**, 94km (58 miles), at 1,185m (3,888ft), is a starting point for treks to the Agoundis Valley, which is less visited than the Toubkal region.

The Nfiss Valley was the stronghold of the powerful Goundafi tribe, and on the left of the road after Ijoukak there is a Goundafi kasbah, now being restored as a hotel. The fortresses of the

Star Attraction
● Mount Toubkal

Trekking in the Atlas
Trekking in the mountains of Morocco is an ideal way of experiencing the stunning landscape of the Atlas and having some first-hand contact with the Berber people. Trekking centres exist in Imlil (Toubkal Massif) and Tabant in the Aït Bougames (Mgoun Masif), where guides, mules, food and village accommodation can be easily organised. The Moroccan Ministry of Tourism produces a very good free information booklet on trekking, listing guides, mountain accommodation and official rates. Contact GTAM, Ministère du Tourisme, Avenue Mohammed V, Quartier des Ministères, Rabat, tel: 037 76 17 01.

In the shadow of Toubkal

High Atlas differ both in appearance and function from the kasbahs of the Draâ and Dades valleys. Built at strategic points to control the all-important caravan passes, they marked the domains of the various *caids*. By the end of the 19th century, Tayeb el Goundafi, one of the three principal lords of the Atlas, could raise an army of 5,000 men.

Below: Berber woman
Bottom: the mosque at Tin-Mal

THE MOSQUE OF TIN-MAL

Signposted off to the right, 4km (2½ miles) after **Ijoukak**, is the 12th-century mosque of ★ **Tin-Mal**, built by the first Almohad caliph, Abd el-Mumin, in 1153. The founder of the Almohads was the charismatic Ibn Tumert, who on appointing Abd el-Mumin as his successor gave him the title 'Amir al-Mumini' ('Commander of the Faithful'), which has been kept by rulers of Morocco ever since. Ibn Tumert was buried at Tin-Mal, which became a place of pilgrimage despite being sacked by the Merinids towards the end of the 13th century. Today the mosque has been greatly restored, but in the north corner, to the left of the *mihrab* (niche indicating the direction of Mecca) a beautifully carved cupola can be seen.

Further along the road, the Goundafi kasbah of **Tagoundaft**, built in 1865 at a height of 1,600m (5,249ft), comes into view.

SUMMIT OF THE PASS

From Idni onwards, the road passes through the Nfiss gorge and spirals up to the ★ **Tizi-n-Test**. From the top of the pass (2,092m/6,863ft), there is a magnificent view of the wide Souss Valley, 200km (124 miles) long and separating the High and the Anti-Atlas.

The southern side of the Atlas is much more barren than the north. For the most part, thorny argan trees are the only vegetation in the desolate landscape; occasionally a quilt of green fields stitched round a few oases brightens the monotony. But down in the valley of the Chleuh Berbers, orange and olive groves stretch to Agadir. At **Aït-**

Yazza, a 24-km (15-mile) detour can be made to **Tiouate**, a little oasis dominated by an old kasbah, the former residence of the *caid*.

TAROUDANNT

★★**Taroudannt** (pop. 57,000), 223km (139 miles), is set spectacularly against the backdrop of the Atlas Mountains, which in the winter are covered in snow. Its pale red city wall was built under the regency of Moulay Ismail. The high clay wall has five gates and almost surrounds the whole town. The Hotel Salam, set into the ramparts, formed a part of the original kasbah.

Historically, Taroudannt served as a staging post for dynasties on the road to power, and in the 16th century it enjoyed a brief reputation as the capital of the Saadians. In 1912 it was the stronghold of El Hiba, the 'Blue Sultan', who led a short-lived revolt against the French protectorate. The main squares of the medina, Place Al-Alaouyine, Place Talmeklat and Place Jotia, have plenty of cheap hotels and cafés.

Taroudannt has an excellent souk. Though it is not as extensive as the one in Marrakech, the individualistic crafts on offer make it an enjoyable and easy place through which to wander.

From Taroudannt it is a straightforward drive along the P32 to Agadir.

> **Royal retreat**
> Outside Taroudannt, on the road to Amezgou, is the Gazelle d'Or (tel: 04 8852039), one of the most exclusive hotels in Morocco. Once the home of a French baron, it is famous for its huge gardens and tasteful interior decor. Patronised mostly by wealthy Europeans, it cultivates a country-club atmosphere and regularly attracts international celebrities and royalty.

Taroudannt city wall

Map
on pages
76–7

10: The Northwest Coast

Casablanca – Rabat – Larache – Asilah – Tangier (372km)

Morocco is not usually thought of as a green country. However, along the Atlantic coastal flats are extensive orange, sugarbeet and sugar cane plantations, green carpets of peanut fields, and in August thousands of sunflowers turning their plate-sized heads towards the sun.

This route north of Casablanca passes through one of the most fertile and also densely populated regions in Morocco. The highlights of the journey are the fortified coastal settlements of Asilah and Larache.

Two to three days should be allowed for this route. There is a choice of two roads: the busy P1 running through the towns of Bouznika, Skhirat and Témara, with side roads branching off to the beaches; and the motorway (small toll), which runs up as far as Larache. Between Casablanca *(see page 29)* and Rabat a narrow coast road offers a third alternative.

CITY SUBURBS

In high summer there is heavy traffic on the coast road, as many wealthy Casablancais have holiday homes by the beaches. After the drab indus-

Below: village door in Asilah
Bottom: sunflowers bloom

trial suburbs, the palm-lined avenues of the harbour town of **Mohammedia**, 28km (17 miles) from Casablanca, make a refreshing change, in spite of some pollution from petrochemical plants. Apart from the beach, there is an 18-hole golf course, marina, casino and race track. Better beaches are found further north at **Skhirat**. The royal palace here was the scene of a failed coup against King Hassan II in 1971 *(see panel right)*.

Situated 11km (7 miles) north of Rabat is Morocco's main zoo (**Parc Zoologique National de Rabat**; open daily 10am–5.30pm). In addition to Barbary apes and camels, it has several Atlas lions. The last wild Atlas lion was shot during the 1920s, but in 1999 a project was launched which, it is hoped, will eventually return the species to the wild.

TO KENITRA

The section of the motorway from Rabat *(see page 22)* to Kenitra passes through the Mamora Forest, a vast forest of cork oaks, acacias and eucalyptus trees *(see page 86)*, but there is more to see on the old road close to the coast.

Nine kilometres (5 miles) north of Salé is the **Jardin Exotique de Rabat-Salé** (open daily 10am–5.30pm), laid out during the protectorate by the French. Now rather neglected, the garden can only be negotiated on marked paths; nonetheless the walk round is a delightful adventure for adults and children alike.

A detour via Mehdiya-Plage follows side roads round the southern tip of the **Lac Sidi-Bourhaba**, a 600-hectare (1,500-acre) protected wetlands site for waders and water birds. The nearby **Mehdiya-Plage** on the estuary of the Sebou river is a popular spot on summer weekends. The ruined kasbah, high above the outer harbour, was built at the end of the 17th century by Moulay Ismail to control the navigable estuary.

Kenitra (pop. 292,000), 133km (83 miles), on a bend of the Sebou river, is the only inland harbour in Morocco. The main products shipped from here are ores, molasses and paper. Built by

The Great Escape
It was in the palace at Skhirat in 1971, while celebrating his 42nd birthday, that King Hassan II faced the first of two serious attempted coups by the army. Nearly 100 guests were gunned down by 1,400 non-commissioned cadets, but the King managed to escape assassination by hiding in a bathroom in a corner of the sprawling palace.

Cork oaks flourish

Map below

the French in 1913, it is an industrial and administrative town with no tourist attractions of note.

THE FERTILE RHARB

Melons for sale in the Rharb

The **Rharb**, north of the Sebou river, is Morocco's most technologically advanced agricultural area. The fertile alluvial soil is ideal for growing early vegetables for export, oil plants for the production of cooking oil, cereals, sugar cane and sugarbeet, and for raising cattle and sheep. **Souk-el-Arba-du-Rharb**, 211km (131 miles), is a popular stopping place for long-distance lorries, cars and buses. Simple grill restaurants flank both sides of the through road, offering excellent grilled lamb, salads and soft drinks. The souk held every Wednesday is an important regional market.

LARACHE AND LIXUS

On the Spanish-looking Place de la Libération of **Larache** (pop. 90,000), 284km (176 miles), which most tourists drive through on their way to

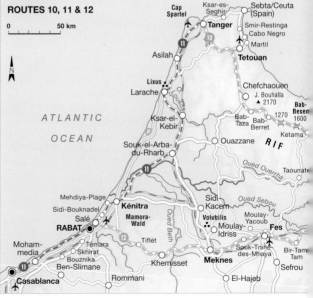

ROUTES 10, 11 & 12

nearby Lixus *(see below)*, are a number of pleasant terrace cafés and restaurants. From this square, roads lead to the new town as well as to the medina and souk. A winding alley leads to the **Archaeological Museum**, in the former palace of Sultan Youssef Abdelhak el-Merini (1258–81), displaying ancient finds from Lixus, including a collection of coins.

★ **Lixus** is the second most important excavation of a classical site in Morocco after Volubilis. Originally founded by the Phoenicians in about 1100BC, from AD40 to the 5th century it was a thriving Roman trading centre. With 10 fish-salting establishments, it was the largest salting centre in the colony of Mauritania Tingitana.

On the left side of the road are the foundation walls of the 147 basins where salted fish and garum paste from anchovies were produced for Rome. A footpath leads up onto the hill platform and the ruins of the upper town, in which rows of seats from the amphitheatre and temple foundations have been excavated. In the baths next to the theatre, there is a beautiful floor mosaic

> **The Phoenicians**
> Phoenicians from Tyre, in Lebanon, began to explore the Moroccan coast from around 1100BC, and by around 800BC had developed significant settlements in Lixus (Larache), Tingis (Tangier) and Sala (Chellah, Rabat), exporting agricultural produce, minerals and animal skins. By 500BC the Phoenician cities had fallen under the rule of Carthage in modern-day Tunisia.

Map on pages 76–7

with the expressive head of Oceanus, the god of the sea. Many of the floor mosaics from the merchants' houses have been removed and transferred to the museum in Tetouan (*see page 80*).

Although little has remained of ancient Lixus, its location controlling the estuary and the hinterland of the Oued Loukos is impressive. It was this fertile plain that the ancient Greeks believed to be the site of the gardens of the Hesperides, where grew the mythical golden apples that gave those who ate them eternal youth. Lixus is also supposed to be the place where Hercules won a wrestling match with the Libyan giant Anteus, the mythical founder of the city of Tangier.

ASILAH

Asilah (pop. 25,000), 325km (202 miles), founded by the Phoenicians, was a Portuguese and then Spanish enclave from 1471–1589, at which point it was ceded to the Saadian Sultan Moulay Ahmed Mansour. The Riffian outlaw, El Raisuli (famous for having kidnapped Walter Harris, the correspondent of the London *Times*, and depicted in a Hollywood film by Sean Connery) built a palace here in 1909.

Today, the old white walled town retains much of its Portuguese character, although its harbour is somewhat empty and forlorn. The Thursday souk is particularly picturesque and the Portuguese wall, entered by Bab el Kasaba, conceals a charming old town centre. Just around the corner from the gate, the seafront has several licensed fish restaurants, including Chez Garcia and Pepe's. North of town there is a fine beach, overlooked by a few roadside hotels.

Thanks to Mohammed Benaissa, and his school friend Mohammed Melhi, both accomplished artists, the town has become a centre for artists. In August, the town holds a cultural festival, during which artists are encouraged to cover walls of the medina streets with brightly coloured murals. Raisuli's palace is used to house important guests at the festival, and has artists' studios, with a fine art printing press attached.

Below: Roman remains, Larache
Bottom: Asilah fisherman

11: The Rif Mountains

Tangier – Tetouan – Chefchaouen – Al-Hoceima – Oujda (628km/390 miles)

Map on pages 76–7

East of Tangier, the P38 to Tetouan rises steadily towards the Rif, a mountain range that reaches 1,600m (5,250ft) at its highest point. Large areas of the range are covered with cork oaks, cedars and pines, which in winter are white with snow. There are relatively few villages in the Rif, and mule paths wind up to isolated farms.

As well as its beautiful scenery, the area is a centre for the cultivation of marijuana (known locally as *kif*). For some time the government, under pressure from Europe, has been trying to clamp down on production and persuade farmers to replace it with other crops. However, this is a hugely profitable industry in an area that suffers from grinding poverty, and the reality is that the area under cultivation is expanding.

A large security force operates in the region to combat illegal drug dealing. You are strongly advised against buying hashish, the narcotic drug derived from the plant. If caught with the substance you could be imprisoned in dismal conditions for up to five years.

With overnight stops in Tetouan, the mountain town of Chefchaouen and Al-Hoceima on the coast, this route takes three to four days by car.

Below: steep village streets
Bottom: the eastern Rif

Map on pages 76–7

From Tangier *(see page 56)* it is only 57km (35 miles) to ★ **Tetouan** (pop. 280,000). In the summer the town is a stopping-off point for many expatriate Moroccans returning home via Ceuta or Tangier for their annual holiday.

SPANISH-FLAVOURED TETOUAN

No other town in northern Morocco has such pronounced Spanish features as Tetouan, the former capital of the Spanish Protectorate. Place Hassan II, where a royal palace was built on the site of the old Caliphate palace, looks distinctly Andalusian.

Below and bottom: haystacks in the Rif Mountains

The medina, founded in the 16th century by refugees from Al-Andalus, is enlivened by good souks, selling everything from quality crafts to cheap electrical goods that have been smuggled through Ceuta. A **Museum of Moroccan Arts** by Bab el-Okla has a comprehensive collection of the region's arts, crafts and costumes, and the **Archaeological Museum** (Place el Jala; 9am–noon, 2.30–5.30pm; closed Tues) displays finds from Morocco's Roman sites, including mosaic floors brought here from Lixus *(see page 77)*.

North of Ceuta, a road (very busy in summer) links the resorts of Martil, Cabo Negro, Mdiq and Smir-Restinga. They all have excellent sandy beaches flanked by club-type holiday complexes.

CHEFCHAOUEN

★★ Chefchaouen (pop. 31,000), 121km (75 miles), is the most attractive town in the Rif. Its blue and white medina is a small maze of pretty alleyways and whitewashed yards. At a height of 520–760m (1,700–2,500ft), the town is dwarfed by the 2,000-m (6,500-ft) mountains rising steeply behind the town.

Chefchaouen was founded in 1471 by Reconquista refugees from Al-Andalus under the leadership of Moulay Ali Ben Rachid, whose tomb in the town attracts pilgrims to this day. Until the early 20th century, Christians were forbidden from entering Chefchaouen; when they eventually did under the Spanish Protectorate they were amazed to find a community of Jews, descended from the first refugee settlers, speaking 10th-century Castilian, a language extinct in Spain for over 400 years.

Today, Chefchaouen prospers on the pilgrim trade, tourism and the sale of craft products. The principal street of the medina (follow the main thrust of the pedestrian traffic) leads into Outa el-Hammam, the main square of the old town, where a string of low-key restaurants are shaded by mulberry trees. On the southeast side of the square is the **Grand Mosque**, one of the town's earliest buildings (only its octagonal minaret is not original), and the kasbah, built by Moulay Ismail. Jebali Berber women, wearing their distinctive straw hats and red-and-white striped *ftouh* (wraps) figure prominently at the markets held on Mondays and Thursdays.

KETAMA AND AL-HOCEIMA

A string of small, expanding market towns punctuate the pass road as it climbs towards **Ketama**. This town is set in the midst of the largest kif-growing area in Morocco, but it is also a modest winter sports resort and a springboard for hikes into the **Tidiquin Massif** (2,448m/8,031ft).

From Ketama the road spirals down to **Al-Hoceima** (pop. 55,000) on the Mediterranean coast, 334km (208 miles). The beaches and small

Star Attraction
● Chefchaouen

Riffian Pottery
The terracotta pottery of the Rif is becoming increasingly collectable. The characteristic geometrical black line decorations are found on a variety of forms ranging from small double-handled pots with elegant dipped lips to *tajine* pots, water jars and butter urns. Modern examples can be bought in small rural market towns across the region at a fraction of the cost of the antique pots sold to serious collectors.

Souvenirs for sale in Chefchaouen

Map on pages 76–7

Zegzel Gorge

rocky bays are popular with Moroccans and Spaniards but out of season it is quiet.

Heading inland again, the road winds uphill along the Nekor valley, where lush vegetation grows in the fertile soil of the wide river bed. The new settlements that have grown up around the old market sites such as Midar or Driouch have few attractions, and **Nador** (pop. 112,000), 488km (303 miles), the provincial capital, has no sights of interest. Further east, in the alluvial plain of the Oued Moulouya, in the midst of large orange groves, is the agricultural centre of **Berkane**, which is also the source of the Beni-Snassen wines.

THE BENI-SNASSEN MASSIF

To the south of Berkane it is possible to make a detour (round trip of 138km/86 miles) into the **Beni-Snassen Massif**, which rises to a height of 1,532m (5,026ft). The porous limestone mountains were named after a powerful Berber tribe that had already settled here prior to the spread of Islam. There are two caves to visit: in the prehistoric **Grotte du Pigeon** ('Cave of the Dove'), archaeologists found two necropolises with 180 human skeletons dating from between the 20th and the 8th millennia BC. The other cave, the **Grotte du Chameau**, contains a stalagmite in the shape of a camel.

This circuit passes through the scattered village of **Sidi-Bouhria**, the mountain village of **Taforalt** (Wednesday souk) and the richly cultivated ★ **Gorges du Zegzel**, before returning to Berkane.

From here, the route turns south to **Oujda** (pop. 350,000), 628km (390 miles), the most important town in eastern Morocco, next to the Algerian border. Fought over for centuries by Berbers, Arabs and Turks, the town was eventually pacified by the French. The town has no important monuments and since the closure of the border with Algeria and the subsequent loss of cross-border trade, it has a rather neglected air. Algerian influences are discernible in Oujda's dialect, music and women's dress.

12: The Sultans' Road

Oujda – Fes – Meknes – Rabat (550km/342 miles)

Map on pages 76–7

The high points of this route are the imperial cities of Fes, Meknes and Rabat (each covered in earlier chapters). Nevertheless, there is plenty to interest the visitor between the cities. The scenery is pastoral: steppe with grazing sheep, silvery olive groves, and citrus plantations in the Sebou basin. With overnight stays in Taza, Fes (two nights) and Meknes, five days should be allowed for the journey by car.

THE TAZA GAP

The Taza Gap, the narrow corridor between the Rif and Middle Atlas, has been an area of conflict since Roman times. And not without reason: all the invaders from the east used this relatively easy passage on their campaigns of conquest. It was also an important conduit for trade, and Berbers from the Benni-Snassen tribe would lie in wait to ambush the caravans. The area is still strategically important and has heavy concentrations of Moroccan military.

The grey ribbon of asphalt runs in a straight line across the plain. The kasbahs – many of them built by Moulay Ismail in the 17th century – are relics from the days of armed conflict and plunder.

Below: drawing water
Bottom: the Chika Gorge in the Tazzekka National Park

Map on pages 76-7

On Tuesdays it is worth stopping at **El-Aioun**, 59km (37 miles) from Oujda, for the weekly souk, which is attended by members of many different Berber tribes. The town has a military kasbah with a mosque built during the reign of Moulay Ismail.

Pepper trees line the streets of the new town of **Taourirt** (110km/68 miles). Until the early 20th century the original town, 5km (3 miles) to the northwest, was contained within the walls of the kasbah, built by Moulay Ismail on a junction of the caravan routes from Sijilmassa in the Tafilalet to Melilla and from the east to the Maghreb.

West of here, on the sparsely vegetated steppe, graze the sheep of the Haouara tribe. The countryside doesn't turn green again until the road approaches **Guercif**, 162km (101 miles), on the Oued Moulouya.

TAZA

The attraction of **Taza** (pop. 120,000), 227km (141 miles), is its isolation from the usual tourist routes. Though significant historically – for centuries, it was only the possession of Taza, and with it the important east-west passage, that guaranteed control over Fes – the majority of its monuments are religious and cannot be visited by non-Muslims; as a result it is refreshingly free of souvenir shops.

Below: the Gouffre de Friouato
Bottom: rooftop view, Taza

The Almohads captured the city from the Almora-vides in 1141–2, and made it their second capi-tal after Tin-Mal. In 1914, the French established a garrison on the plateau below the town and from here master-minded the defeat of the Rif rebellion led by Abd-el-Krim *(see page 17)*.

The new town, situated 2km (1½ miles) north-east of the old town, is rather drab. By contrast, the medina is still enclosed by a wall and has a number of features dating from the Almohad era. Visitors usually begin a tour of the medina at the Bab Jemaa on the east side, leading into Rue Nej-jarine, the south–north artery of the old town. The route passes the Mausoleum of Sidi Azouz, the patron saint of Taza, and a Moorish wall fountain, to the Great Mosque on the northern edge, parts of which pre-date the mosque at Tin-Mal *(see page 72)*. From the Bab er-Rih in the northern wall there is a fine view of the lower town.

> **Refreshment stop**
> It is a good idea to take a picnic into the Tazzeka National Park (picnic tables pro-vided). Alternatively, the little village of Ras el Ma, halfway down Jbel Tazzeka, has a superbly-sited rustic café where it is possible to sip mint tea and admire the view of Taza in the gap between the Middle Atlas and hills of the eastern Rif to the north.

TAZZEKA NATIONAL PARK

After Taza, a detour of 76km (47 miles) can be made through the ★ **Tazzeka National Park**, the most impressive section of this route. The 12,700-hectare (31,400-acre) national park is home to boar, jackals, red foxes, red deer and birds of prey. Cork, holm, turkey and kermes oaks, thujas and oleanders cover the slopes; the magnificent cedar forest on the **Jbel Tazzeka** (1,980m/6,260ft) is a protected area.

Even though you will probably not see any ani-mals, the trip itself is very worthwhile. There are several notable caves; the **Grottes du Chiker** cannot be visited, but you can enter the **Gouf-fre de Friouato**, a dripstone cave explored to a depth of 305m (1,000ft) and length of 2,221m (7,287ft). The top section can be visited in the company of a guide, who will take you down the 512 steps to a depth of 180m (590ft).

After you have traversed the passes of Bab-Bou-Idir and Bab-Taka, a wooded road branches off to the summit of Jbel Tazzeka. In winter, this stretch is frequently unpassable, and even in the summer it is often only negotiable with a four-

Taza flock

Map on pages 76–7

Sefrou
About 30km (20 miles) southeast of Fes, amongst the foothills of the Middle Atlas, is the ancient city of Sefrou. It was once home to Morocco's most concentrated Jewish population, which has left its mark in the many wooden balconied houses of the old town. The attractive walled pedestrian medina, set astride the Aggal river, comes to life each Thursday when farmers from the surrounding hills come to town for its weekly market.

Roadside shrine

wheel drive. Continue down through dense cork oak forests, and the winding 10km- (6 mile-) long Oued Zireg gorge to rejoin the main road at the scattered settlement of Sidi-Abdallah-des-Rhiata.

THE SEBOU BASIN

As the road rises towards the Bir-Tam-Tam (578m/ 1,896ft), 304km (189 miles), there is a view of the massive **Idriss I reservoir** on the Oued Sebou. Cereals, citrus fruits and olives thrive in the rich black soil of the area. The road then spirals down into the Sebou basin towards Fes *(see page 41)*.

FES TO RABAT

From Fes, a new motorway runs west to Rabat, with a turn-off for Meknes, but you may want to take the slower route. The plateau between the two imperial cities is predominantly agricultural, with vineyards covering the low hills around Meknes. The main roads running through the small market towns are lined with simple but usually good grill restaurants, where you can stop for charcoal-grilled lamb.

The imperial city of **Meknes** *(see page 34)* can be seen from a considerable distance.

Beyond Meknes, **Khemisset** (pop. 100,000) is the rapidly growing capital of the province of the same name. This agricultural centre in the territory of the Zemmour Berbers has a reputation for producing fine carpets.

After **Tiflet**, 494km (307 miles), the route passes through the largest cork oak forest in Morocco, the **Mamora Forest**, a sandy area extending 60km by 40km (37 miles by 25 miles). The trees are interspersed with pine and mimosa, and in March and April the mimosa blossom turns the area a vivid yellow. The road finally crosses the Hassan II Bridge to enter the capital **Rabat**, 550km (342 miles) *(see page 16)*. If you arrive at dusk, you can't miss the Mausoleum of Mohammed V and the nearby Tour Hassan which are illuminated on the skyline.

13: A Trans-Atlas Journey

Fes – Ifrane – Azrou – Er Rachidia – Erg Chebbi – Rissani (478km/297miles)

Map on page 88

The contrasts along this route could hardly be greater. After the winter sports resorts of the Middle Atlas, such as Imouzzèr or Ifrane, which bear certain resemblances to their counterparts in central Europe, the scene changes dramatically at Midelt, where the road drops down over the High Atlas to the south and the palm-filled oasis of the Tafilalet. This trans-Atlas tour culminates spectacularly in the reddish-golden dunes of the Erg Chebbi.

For the Fes–Rissani route at least two days are necessary, including stops.

WATERFALLS AND CEDAR FORESTS

South of Fes *(see page 41)*, apple and pear orchards give way to the pine and cedar-clad uplands of the Middle Atlas, where cool summer temperatures and good infrastructure attract well-to-do city dwellers in search of second homes. The area is perceptibly wealthy, especially around Azrou and Ifrane; in winter there is a small winter sports industry at Mischliffen.

The area also has a number of natural springs. Only 38km (24 miles) from Fes, at a height of

Below: market produce
Bottom: where mountains meet the desert

Map below

1,350m (4,429ft), is the health resort of **Imouzzer-du-Kandar**, in the shadow of the summit of the same name. This tidy town with its fruit trees and pools makes a delightful, low-key base for exploring the Middle Atlas.

IFRANE

Ifrane, at a height of 1,650m (5,413ft), 63km (39 miles) from Fes, is rather more chic. Red-tiled villas and chalets belonging to the well-off are

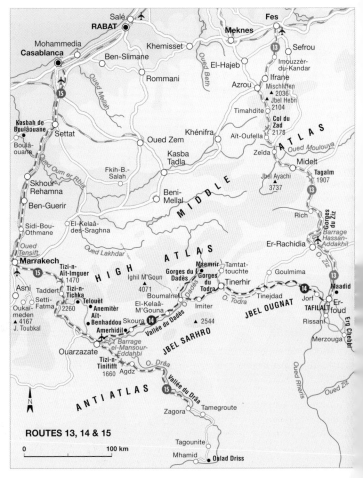

ROUTES 13, 14 & 15

0   100 km

concealed in large gardens. On the far side of town the road passes a royal château, which was a favourite residence of Hassan II.

Ifrane was founded in 1929 by French settlers who owned large estates in the triangle formed by Meknes, Fes and Ifrane; they came here to ski, hunt and fish. Today, Ifrane is the most popular winter sports area next to Oukaïmeden *(see page 55)*. The ski slopes lie 17km (11 miles) to the south of the town, at Mischliffen (2,036m/6,680ft) and Jbel Hebri (2,104m/6,903ft).

In 1994 Hassan II founded the university of Al-Akhawayn, modelled on American colleges. To cater for the three monotheistic religions, a mosque, a synagogue and a church were built on the campus: they stand as symbols of the 'tolerant Islam' promoted by the Moroccan royal family.

> **Lake district**
> A few kilometres south of Imouzzer-du-Kandar is the start of the lakes tour, passing lakes Aoua, Aforgah, Iffer, Ifrah and Hachlat, via a series of tiny tarmaced roads each reasonably signposted. Many of the lakes offer good fishing, and accommodation can be found in the Chalet du Lac (tel: 055 66 31 97) and the Gite du Dayet Aoua (tel: 055 60 48 80). The eastern side of the lakes region is bordered by the P20, which leads north to Sefrou.

AZROU

Azrou (pop. 41,000), at a height of 1,250m (4,100ft), is an important market centre for the Beni-Mguild Berbers, who inhabit a large area in the central Middle Atlas (some of them still live a semi-nomadic life and you may see their dark-brown tents in the valleys).

As you approach Azrou from the north, the green-tiled minaret of the Hassan I Mosque is the first thing that comes into view. In the western part of town are the remnants of a 17th-century kasbah, and in the centre of town is the volcanic outcrop from which Azrou gets its name. Here, painted in Arabic script, are the three determining elements in the life of every Moroccan: God (top), nation (right) and king (left).

Azrou is famous for its carpets and cedarwood carvings, which are sold in the Coopérative Artisanale. Its carpet factory is also open to visitors.

VOLCANIC UPLANDS

Past the rough-stone houses of **Timahdite** (1,815m/5,955ft), a place popular with mountaineers, the route continues across a high plateau of volcanic origin, with the Col du Zad, at 2,178m

Landscape of cedars between Ifrane and Azrou

Map on page 88

Arab Island
The people of the Tafilalet are very different from the communities inhabiting the Dades and the Draa to the west. The home territory of the Alaouite dynasty, the Tafilalet is an isolated Arab community whose roots in the valley are far older than those of the Berber tribes surrounding them today.

The desert at Merzouga

(7,146ft), marking its highest point. From Aït-Oufella onwards (155km/96 miles) the view to the south is dominated by the towering ramparts of the 3,737-m (12,260-ft) Jbel Ayachi; for months its long ridge is covered in snow. **Midelt** (pop. 39,000), 205 km (127 miles), at a height of 1,488m (4,882ft), is a busy market town, with several hotels. It has a well respected carpet cooperative and is a good place to buy gemstones and minerals found in the mountains here.

DESCENT TO THE DESERT

It is only after the Tagalm Pass (1,907m/6,257ft) that the road starts its descent down the bare lee side of the High Atlas onto the high plateau of the pre-Sahara. After the little town of Rich, the road follows the winding course of the river Ziz, running through the beautiful ★★ **Ziz Gorge**. The views are superb: red cliffs contrast with splashes of greenery – argan trees, tamarisks, palms, rich green fields – and clay-built villages.

The route continues past the Barrage of Hassan-Addakhil to **Er-Rachidia** (pop. 62,000), 346km (215 miles) at the crossroads of the major roads from the Atlantic to Algeria and from central Morocco to the Sahara Desert. The town developed around a French garrison and is still the main administrative centre of the region. It has nothing special to offer, but it is nonetheless a pleasant place to spend the night.

THE TAFILALET

The main road south runs along the Ziz Valley, linking a string of oases with thousands of date palms. The route is lined with the clay-coloured *ksour (see page 106)* typical of the region. Such villages, a common sight in Morocco, are surrounded by a protective wall with fortified towers up to 12m (39ft) high, with a main gate, also flanked by towers, and a labyrinth of alleyways.

A few kilometres south of Er-Rachidia is the so-called 'Source Bleu' of **Meski**, the other river of the Ziz. What was once an idyllic oasis centring on a series of pools has lost a lot of its character; the pools now have cement bottoms and are surrounded by a café and souvenir stalls.

ERFOUD AND THE ERG CHEBBI

Erfoud (pop. 18,000), 425km (264 miles), was also originally a garrison, established by the French in 1917 to control the nearby border territory. The Tafilalet was once the main market for trade caravans in southeast Morocco. Today, the town's inhabitants live from oasis farming, breeding sheep and tourism. If you want to buy fossils, you will find some fine specimens at the Sahara-Sea-Collection, opposite the Hotel Tafilalet on the main road through town.

Erfoud is the main base for trips to the dramatic sand dunes of ★★**Erg Chebbi**, the highest in Morocco (up to 100m/328ft). It is worth spending at least one night in one of the simple hotels beneath the dunes or in a tent, as only then can you experience the magnificent play of colours across the sand at sunrise and sunset.

The road to Erg Chebbi is tarmac for 17km (11 miles) then a track for a further 36km (22 miles), culminating in the oasis of **Merzouga**. Visitors may prefer to negotiate the myriad tracks with the help of a guide, easily hired in Erfoud or Rissani. However, orientation is easy once you

Star Attractions
● Ziz Gorge
● Erg Chebbi

Below: desert vehicle, Erfoud
Bottom: Ziz Valley Kasbah

Map on page 88

In search of a date
Rissani is said to be one of the world's largest date *palmeries*, with some 4 million trees and more than 100 varieties of dates. Travel through the region in October and you will find the date harvest in full swing.

see the red dunes in the distance, contrasted against the stony desert of the approach. Although small in size, the Erg Chebbi does offer a taste of the classic Saharan landscape; it has been used as a location for a number of films, including *Lawrence of Arabia*.

As well as climbing the dunes, visitors to Merzouga can walk around the village, meet the locals and check out the **Depot Nomade**, the proprietor of which delights in explaining some of the symbolism behind the patterns of the Berber carpets on sale. There is little pressurised salesmanship here, and the prices are fair – a refreshing change from many such outlets in Morocco.

THE END OF THE ROAD

A few hundred metres outside **Rissani**, the red clay walls of the ancient trading town of **Sijilmassa** rise out of the sand. Until the 14th century, it was a checkpoint for the caravans passing through to Timbuktu in Mali. When Rissani took over as the main town of the Tafilalet, Sijilmassa gradually disappeared beneath the sand; excavation work is in progress.

At the end of the Tafilalet, Rissani is one of Morocco's great trading crossroads. It is famous for its market, a continuous mêlée of haggling and jostling, where enormous trucks compete with laden donkeys. It is certainly the most African market in Morocco.

In addition, Rissani is an important pilgrimage centre, based on the tomb of Moulay Ali Sherif (closed to non-Muslims), the founder of Morocco's ruling Alaouite dynasty. Descended from Hassan, the son of Ali and Fatima (daughter of the Prophet Mohammed), the Alaouite sherifs settled in the Tafilalet by the 13th century, reinvigorating the ancient city of Sijilmassa. The Alaouites came to power in 1666 when Moulay Rachid was proclaimed sultan in Fes.

Behind the *zaouia* (mausoleum) are the ruined remains of the Alaouite Ksar Akbar, one of several Alaouite kasbahs dotting the area; unlike the *zaouia*, it is open to non-Muslims.

Rissani, a trading crossroad

14: Valley of a Thousand Kasbahs

Erfoud – Gorges du Todra – Gorges du Dades – El-Kelaâ M'Gouna – Skoura – Ouarzazate (311km/193 miles)

This route passes through some of the most dramatic scenery in Morocco. On one side rises the High Atlas range, with jagged, often snow-capped peaks soaring to between 3,000–4,000m (10,000–13,000ft); on the other are the magnificent but barren 2,500-m (8,000-ft) summits of the Jbel Sarhro. Cutting into the Atlas are the Todra and Dades gorges.

Along the main valley and part way into the gorges, oases line the river courses and red clay *ksour (see page 106)* blend into river terraces, glowing red in the late afternoon sun.

The exotic beauty of the so-called 'Valley of a Thousand Kasbahs' makes it a memorable journey for every traveller in Morocco. Overnight stays in Tinerhir, Boumalne or El-Kelaâ M'Gouna are recommended. Two to three days should be allowed to complete the journey.

WEST OF ERFOUD

From Erfoud *(see page 91)* the route strikes west, passing through a string of oases with half-ruined clay villages and kasbahs. On the other side of

*Below: Gorges de Dades
Bottom: the High Atlas above the Gorge*

Map
on page
88

Jorf, the otherwise flat desert plateau is studded with huge mounds concealing entrances to ancient irrigation channels which, fed from the ground water, supplied the oases with fresh water until they sanded up. During the disastrous drought of 1994–5, the oasis farmers remembered their pipelines and dug some of them out of the sand.

TINEJDAD

Below: gathering brushwood
Bottom: Tinerhir

In **Tinejdad**, the administrative centre of the Fer-kla oases, the route joins the main road from Er-Rachidia to Ouarzazate, otherwise known as the Valley of the Kasbahs. **Asrir**, a *ksar (see page 106) a*bout 5km (3 miles) west of Tinejdad, is one of the most interesting in the area. The women, mostly Haratines, wrap themselves in blue-black *haïks* decorated with colourful embroidery.

A detour of 24km (15 miles) each way can be made to **Goulmima**, north of Tinejdad on the Oued Rheris. The old Goulmima *ksar*, 1½km (1 mile) east of the town, has been restored and has an impressive main gate 14m (46ft) deep with three turns and high towers.

TINERHIR

Halfway between Erfoud and Ouarzazate is **Tinerhir**. Situated near the mouth of the Todra

Gorge at a height of 1,342m (4,402ft), this is the administrative centre for the 72 *ksour* in the area. Tinerhir has an important market and is prosperous, being a popular domicile for Moroccans returning from abroad. It is well-known for its gold and silver jewellery workshops and castellated buildings. Its souk is held on Monday, but on any day of the week the local produce can be sampled at the simple restaurants around the central market square: simply order what you want from a butcher and grocer and it will be cooked for you on a charcoal grill.

The oases around the town are attractive places to stop. Here, Aït-Atta Berbers, Chorfa Arabs, Haratines and other tribes eke out a living from oasis farming, growing dates, olives, almonds, figs, pomegranates and grapes.

TODRA GORGE

Tinerhir is the starting point for a detour into the impressive ★★**Todra Gorge**. After about 13km (8 miles) you come to its narrow entrance, only 10m (33ft) wide, flanked by soaring, 300-m (980-ft) cliffs. These are always a popular spot for climbers and you may see some inching their way up the rock walls.

Though the gorge is accessible in an ordinary hire car, and parts of the new piste have been raised above the river bed, you may feel more secure in a four-wheel drive vehicle, especially after a rainy spell when the water will probably be knee-deep. It is important to keep an eye on weather conditions, as after heavy rains the gorge is susceptible to dangerous flash floods. Be that as it may, the Todra is on the tour-bus route, and you may get stuck behind one as you drive through.

The gorge itself is only about 1km (½ mile) long, but has a number of pretty villages as well as a few hotels and restaurants; beyond it, a track leads via the village of Tamtattouchte deep into the Atlas Mountains to Agoudal and Imilchil *(see panel)*. This track can only be negotiated by four-wheel drive; it also links up, via various high passes, with the Dades Gorge to the west.

Star Attraction
● Todra Gorge

Wedding festival
The Atlas north of the Todra Gorge, a severely beautiful high-altitude desert, is home to the Aït Haddidou Berbers, one of the country's largest semi-nomadic tribes. The tribe is famous for its annual *moussem* (September), the Marriage Festival near Imilchil. Despite a huge influx of tourists in recent years, the three-day market and festival remains a genuine Berber event with thousands of Berbers coming from the surrounding area to take advantage of the last big market before the onset of winter.

Entrance to the Todra Gorge

Map
on page
88

*Below and bottom:
Boumalne valley*

BOUMALNE

The main route continues from Tinerhir past the kasbahs of **Imiter**, 176km (109 miles) from Erfoud, between the High Atlas range in the north and the Jbel Sarhro in the south.

Boumalne, 195km (121 miles), on the Dades river, is the modern administrative centre of the region and an important market town. On Wednesdays there is a lively souk attended by highland Berbers from the surrounding *ksour*.

The old Boumalne *ksar* has several massive kasbahs, most of which have been deserted by their owners in favour of comfortable new accommodation close by. These modern cement houses have, of course, spoiled the look of the place, and do not have the same insulating benefits – cool in summer, warm in winter – as the *ksour*.

THE DADES GORGE

Boumalne is the starting point for a detour to the **★★ Dades Gorge**. This canyon, around 33km (21 miles) long, contains several old *ksours* such as Aït-Ouffli, Aït-Arbi and Aït-Tamlalt, and offers a wonderful example of architecture blending harmoniously with nature. The scenic beauty of ochre-coloured walls and green valley bottoms, with the snow-capped Atlas as a backdrop, is very hard to beat.

The settled part of the gorge is much longer than the Todra, but unless you have a four-wheel drive vehicle, your end point will probably be the top of the steep-sided ravine; this is surmounted via a series of terrifying switchbacks.

Star Attraction
● Dades Valley

THE DADES VALLEY

The main route to the west continues down the ★★ **Dades Valley**, passing brownish-red outcrops topped by *ksour*. On the last part of the route, *ksour* follow one another at short intervals. **El-Kelaâ M'Gouna**, 219km (136 miles), attracts many visitors in May with its rose festival, featuring processions, dances and the election of a rose queen.

At a height of 1,467m (4,813ft), the date palms peter out, but a wide variety of fruit is grown, including apples, almonds and figs, as well as roses for the French perfume industry. On a cliff on the Asfi-M'Goun bank is a kasbah that was owned by the former *pacha* of Marrakech, the infamous Thami el-Glaoui. **Mont M'Goun** (4,071m/13,356ft), the second-highest peak in Morocco, rises to the north.

The rose plantations extend as far as **Skoura**. There are around 50 *ksour* scattered among the oases hereabouts. A number of the kasbahs have two unusual features: the corner towers are of differing height and width, and the upper parts of the towers are decorated with intricate brick ornamentation. The vast 19th-century kasbah complex of Amerhidil on the right bank of the Oued Hajjaj, about 1km (½ mile) from the main road, is particularly impressive, although it is slowly falling into ruin.

OUARZAZATE

Although the tamarisks lining the entry into the town, by the El-Mansour Eddahbi reservoir, make an attractive start to **Ouarzazate** (pop. 40,000), 311km (193 miles), the town is primarily functional and modern, with a range of hotels and full tourist facilities. It has its origins in a French

> **Legacy of the Legion**
> Ouarzazate originated as a base for the French Foreign Legion. The Legionnaires have left their mark in the church, which is still maintained by Catholic nuns, and the characterful Chez Dimitri restaurant, set up by an energetic Greek who jumped ship in Casablanca as a 14-year-old boy in 1928 and eventually joined the Legion. Once a wild drinking den, Demitri's is now one of the best restaurants south of the Atlas. It is run by Demitri's son.

Amerhidil Kasbah, Skoura

Map on page 88

Below and bottom: interior and exterior of the Glaoui Kasbah, Taourirt

garrison to the west of the clay-walled village of **Taourirt** on the edge of Ouarzazate.

The village is known for the impressive ★★ **Glaoui Kasbah**, one of the largest of the feudal castles of the Glaoui clan, whose famous leader, Thami-el-Glaoui, ruled over a large part of southern Morocco during the time of the French protectorate, extending his sphere of influence by colluding with the French colonisers. Following independence, the El Glaoui clan was left disgraced and dispossessed of their many properties, and these gradually fell into decline. Recently, however, some, including this kasbah, have been partially restored and are now open to the public.

Among Ouarzazate's other facilities are a cultural and congress centre, a film studio and a golf course, not to mention an international airport, all indications of the kind of visitors Ouarzazate attracts. The Royal Golf Course, dating from the early 1990s, is situated next to the reservoir. The clubhouse in kasbah style stands on the shore of the lake, along with a number of luxurious holiday villas belonging to wealthy Moroccans.

FILM INDUSTRY

In recent years Morocco, and particularly the region of Ouarzazate, has become an important location for film-making. The history of the film location business in Morocco goes back to the Lumiere Brothers and such classics as Orson Welles' *Othello* and David Lean's *Lawrence of Arabia*. However, it is recent blockbusters, such as *Romancing the Stone* and *The Mummy,* that have really put Morocco on the film-makers' map, and in the process created a new multi-million industry for the country, employing thousands of locals as extras and technicians.

With the surrounding Atlas scenery being so similar to Tibet, Ouarzazate's film studios (to the north of the town centre) have proved popular among producers of 'Tibet' movies, including, most famously, Martin Scorsese's film, *Kundun*, released in 1998.

15: The Coast to the Desert

Casablanca – Marrakech – Tizi-n-Tichka – Ouarzazate – Agdz – Zagora (605km/376 miles)

Map on page 88

Marrakech, with its Jemaa el-Fna, historic monuments, medina and palm-filled gardens, is the principal city and one of the major highlights of this route *(see page 48)*. However there are many interesting sights on the way to and from Marrakech, particularly on either side of the 4,000-m (13,000-ft) peaks of the High Atlas. Ouarzazate *(see page 97)* is a useful halfway stop on this journey to the desert.

Allow at least three days for this route.

Star Attraction
● **Glaoui Kasbah**

Below: nesting storks
Bottom: Kasbah de Boulâouane

LEAVING CASABLANCA

As essential as the fertile Chaouïa alluvial plain and the phosphate are to the country's economy, from a tourist point of view the stretch between Casablanca *(see pages 22–25)* and Marrakech is rather monotonous.

Of the towns en route, only **Settat** (pop. 96,200) is of interest. A modern agricultural centre, it has also become an industrial and university town, and is now keen to profit from expanding tourism.

A detour (50km/31 miles each way) can be made from Settat to the **Kasbah de Boulâouane**. The road runs through wooded countryside and

Pit stop

Taddert is the last truck stop before the road twists steeply up to the pass, and it is lined with grill cafés. Stop at one of these, or possibly at the Auberge des Noyers, a survivor of the Protectorate period. The auberge has rooms and a walnut shaded terrace at the back where you can drink cold beers.

finally crosses the river Oum er Rbia. The kasbah with its mosque was built by Moulay Ismail in 1710; from the battlements and the minaret there is a splendid view of the fertile valley with the river winding through it.

After Sidi-Bou-Othmane, the main road passes through the Jbilet hills, and soon the Koutoubia minaret, a famous landmark in Marrakech *(see pages 38–43)* comes into view (237km/147km).

INTO THE HIGH ATLAS

Leaving Marrakech for **Ouarzazate** via the Tizi n-Tichka pass, the road crosses the fertile plain south of the city. Lined with eucalyptus and tamarisks and passing olive groves on either side, it is pleasant enough, crossing small tributaries of the Oued Tensift such as the Oued R'Mat and Oued Zate as it climbs to the first pass in the High Atlas, **Tizi-n-Aït-Imguer** (1,470m/ 4,823ft). Olive trees soon give way to holm oaks, and modern housing to tiny villages of rough red stone or clay clinging to the slopes. **Taddert** on the Rdat torrent, already at a height of 1,650m (5,413ft), is surrounded by walnut trees.

Tourism has invaded this area, as is demonstrated by the many teenagers trying to interest travellers in semi-precious stones (amethyst and onyx, in particular) of varying quality. They are

Farming in the High Atlas

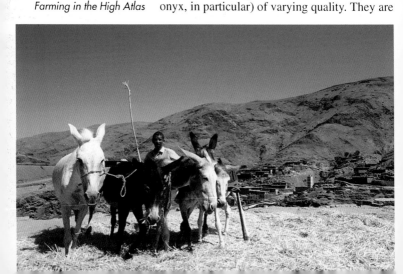

also sold from shops and stalls on the ★★ **Tizi-n-Tichka**. At a height of 2,260m (7,415ft), there is usually a biting wind on this pass, which is surrounded by a wilderness of steep, bare slopes.

TELOUET

On the other side of the pass, a narrow road on the left leads eastwards for 21km (13 miles) to the community of **Telouet**. at the heart of the southern tribal area of the Glaoui Berbers. This powerful tribe once ruled over the entire region southeast of Marrakech, and from the early 19th century controlled important pass roads used by the trans-Atlas traffic.

Here, at a height of 1,800m (5,900ft), surrounded by furrowed red 3,000-m (10,000-ft) peaks, is the ★★ **Dar Glaoui Kasbah**, the former main residence of the Glaoui *caids*. At one time, Telouet was a luxurious palace, staffed with hundreds of retainers and slaves, and it even had a cinema. It played host to Wilfred Thesiger, as well as more unfortunate souls who were left to die shackled deep in its dungeons.

The custodian (if he is not around, one of the children who greet your arrival will be very willing to find him) will open the gates and guide you through the massive complex, which was built in several stages from the mid-19th century onwards. It is not only the size of the kasbah that is impressive, but also the Moorish decoration of the reception rooms.

The Glaoui souk takes place on Thursdays.

DESCENT TO THE SOUTH

The road descends for another 13km (8 miles) to the delightful village of ★ **Anemiter**, situated in a broad green valley on the old caravan route between Aït-Benhaddou and Telouet. Some maps suggest that from here it is easy to continue the journey south for 45km (28 miles) to Aït-Benhaddou. This, however, is not advisable unless you are a very experienced piste driver with a four-wheel drive vehicle.

Star Attractions
● Tizi-n-Tichka
● Dar Glaoui Kasbah, Telouet

Below: view from Telouet
Bottom: inside Telouet

Map
on page
88

It is safer to return to the main road via Telouet and approach Aït-Benhaddou from the south, along a road which forks off north of Ouarzazate.

AIT-BENHADDOU

Set on a steep hillside, the fortified village of ★★★ **Aït-Benhaddou** will be familiar to many people who have never set foot in Morocco, for it has been used as a film location over many years, beginning with Robert Aldrich's 1963 film *Sodom and Gomorrah*, starring Stewart Granger, and more recently featuring as the provincial town in the film *Gladiator*.

Below: keeper of the kasbah
Bottom: Aït-Benhaddou

Local guides will show you around, but it is possible to walk around at leisure, ascending through the maze of alleys to the lookout tower at the top of the hill. Souvenir stalls line the track between the modern centre and old Aït-Benhaddou.

After this detour, continue along the main road to Ouarzazate *(see page 97)*.

GATEWAY TO THE DRAA

Leaving Ouarzazate against the magnificent backdrop of the High Atlas, the road climbs through the stony deserts of the Jbel Tifernine to the pass of Tiz-n-Tinififft (1,660m/5,466ft). To the east, the 2,500-m (8,000-ft) pinnacles of the Jbel Sarho rise above the haze; to the south the road spirals down to the oasis of **Agdz**, known for its carpets, and the first date palms of the ★★★ **Draa Valley** come into view.

Lush date-palm oases, interspersed with the towers of multiple *ksour* and kasbahs, flourish all along the winding course of the Draa. Five kilometres (3 miles) southeast of Agdz, beyond the left bank of the river, is the old *ksar* of **Tamenougalt** with its amazing defensive architecture. Further south, the village of **Tinezouline** is the scene of a colourful market held on Mondays and Thursdays. In this region you are likely to see large numbers of dark-skinned people, whose ancestors were brought to this part of southern Morocco as slaves from the Sudan.

ZAGORA

Zagora (pop. 26,000) is the main market of the south. Nomadic Aït Atta, Saharan Berbers who found their way into Morocco in the 17th century, mix with old Arab families who emigrated from the Arabian peninsula eight centuries ago. Camel caravans from the south used to break their journeys at this point before continuing north and east. A sign saying 'Timbouctou 52 jours' is a playful reminder of the days of the trade caravans.

Zagora's main street is lined with souvenir shops and restaurants, and there are a large number of hotels at all price levels. The town is the starting point for expeditions to the edge of the desert.

From here, it is another 18km (11 miles) to **Tamegroute**, which has an interesting library (open to non-Muslims) in the *zaouia* of the Naciri, a Sufi brotherhood that evolved around the tomb of Sidi M'Hami Ben Nacer. The town is also known for its green-glaze pottery.

From Tamegroute it is another 79km (50 miles) across mostly barren but beautiful terrain to **M'Hamid**; the town's Monday souk sells everything from aphrodisiacs to camels. The young men of the town will guide visitors into the desert, which is mostly stony but occasionally punctuated by impressive sand dunes. Camel safaris are the order of the day.

Star Attractions
- **Aït Benhaddou**
- **Draa Valley**

Desert lodging
At Tinfou, south of Tamegroute, is the characterful Auberge Repos de Sable. Owned by an artist couple living in Rabat, and run by their son, the auberge is a delightful gallery of Moroccan contemporary and folk art.

Tamenougalt, outside Agdz

Architecture

Here the old city, there the new city – wherever you travel in Morocco, the towns and cities are made up of two contrasting parts. Until the French and Spanish protectorates, all Moroccan cities were walled medinas. The colonial powers left these medinas alone, choosing instead to house their administration and settlers in new towns – Villes Nouvelles – outside the walls and built in a colonial style. There was, after all, plenty of room in what was then a thinly populated country, and it was considered important that the culture of the medinas was respected. Space was left between the medinas and the new towns, either by establishing green belts or by siting the new town on the opposite bank of the river.

After the withdrawal of the colonial powers, the richer and more influential families moved out of the cramped medinas into the modern quarters vacated by the Europeans, leaving the medinas to the poor. At the same time, migrants from the countryside poured into the old towns, causing severe overcrowding and a gradual deterioration in their fabric. Although restoration programmes and rehousing projects have been introduced, notably in Fes, progress is slow. Meanwhile, in Fes and Marrakech there is a new trend for wealthy foreigners to buy up medina properties and restore them as second homes – a course that saves the buildings but destroys cultural traditions.

MOORISH ARCHITECTURE

In Arab-occupied Spain between the 9th and 15th centuries, a new style of Islamic architecture developed that became known as the Hispano-Moorish style. Under the Almoravides and the Almohads it spread to Morocco, and reached perfection under the Merinid sultans. The purest form of the Moorish style found expression in sacred buildings, mosques, *madrassas* (Islamic colleges) and mausoleums. Characteristic of this style are the saddle and pyramid roofs and

Modern architecture

The best contemporary Moroccan architecture is stylish and innovative, blending traditional forms with modern tastes and techniques. Some of the finest examples are in Marrakech, where a demand for superb design has been created by the large number of extremely wealthy foreigners with homes in the city. Architects such as Charles Bocarra and Eli Mouyal, an expert in using mud brick technology, have built hotels and private villas that have attracted international acclaim. The new opera theatre in Marrakech, designed by Bocarra, is an ambitious project in a monumental style that incorporates tulip columns inspired by ancient Egyptian temples.

Opposite: the Kasbah at Skoura
Below: Attarine Madrassa, Fes

Valley of the Kasbahs
Fortified villages and castles are still a dominant feature of the landscape from the High Atlas down to the edge of the Sahara, following one another in close succession along the valleys of the desert rivers Ziz, Rheris, Todra, Dades and Draa. It is not without reason that the stretch of country from Ouarzazate to Er-Rachidia is advertised to tourists as the 'Valley of the Thousand Kasbahs'.

canopies with green-glazed tiles. Behind the plain facades stand rectangular courtyards surrounded by arcades, with double doors opening into narrow rooms. The classic form of decoration consist of *zellige* (mosaics of tiny hand-cut glazed tiles). The walls are decorated with arabesques cut into the plaster and calligraphic friezes. The carved wooden ceilings are painted in muted colours.

The style was employed in domestic architecture too. Palaces, houses of the nobility and the reception halls in the kasbahs were built and decorated in a similar if less lavish way, with all ornament internal. However decrepit a traditional town house may appear from the outside, visitors are often surprised by what lies behind the walls. A small gate in a blank wall may lead into a beautiful courtyard, lavishly decorated and perhaps containing a gently trickling fountain.

BERBER ARCHITECTURE

One of the most fascinating forms of architecture in southern Morocco is the *ksar* (plural, *ksour*), a fortified village often inhabited by a single clan, ethnic or social group. A *ksar* usually consists of tall *pisé* (mud-brick) houses built closely together, open or covered mud alleys, a mosque, a *hammam* and storage rooms. Originally the complex was protected by a wall, and the gate kept shut at night. Within the *ksour* there is often a kasbah, a separately fortified building with four corner towers built to accommodate either a garrison or an important family. The upper facades of the tapering towers are often decorated with elaborate geometric patterns.

Below and bottom: Telouet kasbah with interior detail

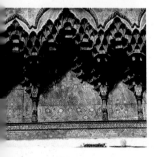

Today, the rather neglected *ksour* are administered from modern centres equipped with administrative buildings, a modern infrastructure and a space for the weekly souk. Each centre administers a certain number of surrounding *ksour*, and usually bears the name of the largest and most important fortified village. The architects of such centres sometimes incorporate traditional motifs in the facades.

The first *ksour* were probably built between the 2nd and 4th centuries, mainly in oases crossed by caravans engaged in the lucrative trade with black Africa. Of the *ksour* that remain today, the oldest date back around 300 years. Only a minority of *ksour* are still inhabited, as the earth bricks weather quickly and need constant maintenance. The fact that these clay castles exist at all is due to the low rainfall of southern Morocco. Unfortunately, many of the deserted *ksour* are falling into ruin.

Below: the Tour Hassan, Rabat
Bottom: zellige (mosaics of hand-cut tiles)

Arts and Crafts

The Moroccans are justly proud of their flourishing craft tradition, as a stroll through any souk will tell you. Colourful carpets, carved furniture, richly embroidered textiles and finely incised brassware all bear the hallmarks of traditional craftsmanship. Arts and crafts are supported by the state, through the establishment of teaching workshops and the creation of co-operatives monitoring quality and price.

In any medina, crafts are grouped according to type, with finer crafts, often relating to luxury goods, located close to the Great Mosque, and smelly or heavy industries, such as tanning, situated on the outskirts. Each craft is organised into a guild, with apprentices working under master craftsmen for several years.

FURNITURE

Morocco has been a major influence on international interior design for several years. Traditional household objects and ornaments are in demand not just for Moroccan homes, but also for export abroad, where *mashrabiya* screens (made of interlocking pieces of wood), colourful carpets and tessellated table tops have become fashionable.

Below: making drums in Fes
Bottom: ceramics salesman in the High Atlas

Azrou, Essaouira, Fes, Marrakech, Meknes, Rabat and Tetouan are all centres for wood-work. Cedar, thuja, oak, walnut, acacia, lemon and ebony are all used. Place Nejjarine in Fes el-Bali is a good place to see woodworking techniques such as marquetry as well as *zawagga* (wood painted in floral and arabesque designs). The old *fondouk* on Place Nejjarine has been turned into a museum of wood-working techniques and tools.

Zellige (mosaics of tiny hand-cut glazed tiles) is an ancient art traditionally employed on walls and floors. The late King Hassan II established several special *zellige* schools.

POTTERY AND METALWORK

Fes, Safi, Marrakech, Salé and Tetouan are renowned for their potteries. Hand-painted *harira* (soup) bowls and communal serving plates are common, as are *tagines*, shallow dishes with conical lids for cooking *tagine* stews.

Copper and brass articles, such as perforated hanging lamps, engraved or damascened plates, candlesticks and incense burners, continue to be popular. A bulbous metal teapot is an essential item of tableware in every home.

LEATHER

Moroccan leather is famous all over the world. At one time whole libraries were sent to Morocco to be morocco-bound. Fes is the best place to see the leather craftsmen at work, but the souks of Marrakech also have a dazzling selection of leather goods. The colourful *babouches* (slippers) make inexpensive and popular presents.

CARPETS AND TEXTILES

Weaving is one of Morocco's oldest and most esteemed craft traditions. Each region produces its own style of carpet. Rabat is a centre for expensive pile carpets, often in red and blue, while the Middle and High Atlas are known for flat-woven *mergoums* in striking geometric designs.

You will also find lengths of hand-woven woollen cloth in cream and browns (sometimes striped), from which men have their winter *jellabas* (long hooded garment) made, and, in the Rif region, *ftouh*, red and white striped cotton wraps. Women's kaftans range from plain wool or cotton outer garments to jewel-encrusted silk gowns for special occasions such as weddings.

Festivals and Events

In addition to the national holidays with their parades and processions, and the religious holidays, which are based on the Islamic Hegira (lunar) calendar, there are national and regional festivals that are well worth experiencing. If you want to visit a festival, ring the tourist office of the place concerned just prior to the event. Sometimes, even annual festivals are cancelled or postponed at short notice.

Berber jewellery
Genuine, individually-made Berber jewellery is very much in demand but also expensive. Look out for *khul khal* (heavy silver anklets) and *fibules*, the elaborate silver pins worn to hold a Berber woman's outer garments in place. The best items are found in the south.

Below: embroidered leather
Bottom: silver jewellery

> ### Moussems
> Moussems, celebrations in honour of national and local holy figures – rulers, leaders of sects and miracle-workers – are legion. Lasting three to seven days, they begin with prayers and sacrifices, and continue with music and dancing, *fantasias* (spectacular feats on horseback) and firework displays. The biggest *moussems* attract visitors from all over Morocco. Equal to their religious importance is the opportunity they present for trade.

Festive gnaoui drummer in the Anti-Atlas

May
Rose Festival in El-Kelaâ M'Gouna (northeast of Ouarzazate). A procession is followed by the election of a rose queen, folk dances and an arts and crafts exhibition.

May/June
Festival of Sacred Music in Fes. Internationally known musicians and orchestras of the three monotheistic religions (Judaism, Christianity and Islam) gather together in the city for an annual festival.

June
Cherry Festival in Sefrou (33km/21 miles southeast of Fes). Cherry festival with folk dances and election of a cherry queen.
Popular Arts Festival in Marrakech. The most important folklore festival in the country. Dance troupes and musicians perform in the floodlit ruins of El Badi Palace. A *fantasia* (feats on horseback) is held every day of the festival.

August
Cultural Festival in Asilah (south of Tangier). International culture week with exhibitions, film shows, lectures and concerts.
Moussem of Moulay Abdallah Amghar, an annual festival in honour of the saint, is held in the coastal town of the same name, south of the resort of El Jadida. A huge complex of tents is erected specially for this *moussem*, which features *fantasias*, falconry and folk dances.

September
Wedding Festival in the remote mountains near Imilchil (province of Er-Rachidia, 130km/81 miles west of the small town of Rich). On a plateau 2,000m (6,600ft) up, the Aït-Haddidou Berbers hold an annual festival in honour of their tribal holy man.

This is also traditionally the occasion when hundreds of brides come to sign the government marriage register, hence its reputation as a wedding festival. There are also folk dances, *fantasias*, a big fair and a cattle market. Overnight accommodation in tents is available.

October
Date festivals *(fêtes des dattes)* are held in the Tafilalet oases around Erfoud. Include folk dances, date souks and the election of a date queen.

December
Festival of Popular Arts in Agadir. Folk dances and many other events celebrating the culture of the deep south.

RELIGIOUS HOLIDAYS

1 Moharrem: Beginning of the Islamic year. One-day festival.
10 Moharrem: Achoura festival (festival of the 10th day). Children are given presents during the celebrations. One-day festival.
Aïd el-Maoulid: the Birthday of the Prophet Mohammed. Two days.
Aïd el-Fitr (also Aïd es-Seghir, 'little festival'): Two-day festival breaking the Ramadan fast. Begins on the first day after the end of Ramadan.
Aïd el-Adha (also Aïd-el-kebir, 'big festival'): Two-day sacrificial festival. The high-point is the ritual slaughtering of a sacrificial ram in memory of Abraham.

Below: moussem *in the Toubkal region*
Bottom: a fantasia in action

FOOD AND DRINK

A RICH MIX OF INFLUENCES

With the immigration of Arabs between the 8th and 10th centuries, new spices and unknown vegetables and ways of preparing them were introduced into Moroccan cuisine. The traditional plain fare of the Berbers – nutritious dishes consisting of wheat, barley, semolina or simple, round flat loaves and mutton – became tastier and more varied with the addition of the new ingredients.

Later on, Spanish and French influences were introduced.

SPECIALITIES

Moroccan cuisine is complex and varied, but you will find most of the following dishes on the menus of almost all restaurants.

Starters include *harira*, a soup made from pulses and lamb or chicken, and thickened with rice; *briouats*, puff pastry squares stuffed with spicy meat, fish or vegetable; and *kbab*, lamb on skewers.

Tagines come in many delicious varieties. A main meal, it consists of chicken, lamb, beef or fish, seasonal vegetables and sometimes fruit or nuts (such as prunes, quinces, olives, apricots, dates or almonds), cooked slowly in a special earthenware dish with a conical lid *(pictured left)*. One of the most popular *tagines*, and often found in restaurants, is *djej maqualli* (chicken with preserved lemons and green olives).

Couscous, the national dish and traditional Friday meal, consists of semolina steamed over vegetables and/or meat.

No festive meal is complete without *pastilla* (top restaurants only). This takes hours to prepare and consists of around 40 layers of translu-cently thin pastry *(warkha)*, filled with ground almonds, chicken or pigeon meat and sprinkled with a dusting of icing sugar.

Liquid sustenance

Mineral water (Sidi Harazem or Oulmes) is sold in all cafés and restaurants. Moroccan wines and beers are sold only in licensed bars and restaurants, almost exclusively in the new towns. At the conclusion of a meal it is traditional to drink mint tea. Hot and very sweet, it is brewed from fresh mint and green or black tea, depending on preference.

RESTAURANT DINING

The vast majority of Moroccans wouldn't dream of eating in a restaurant, unless they were away from home. Restaurant food is generally inferior and by local standards expensive. Those who do eat out – the wealthy middle classes – tend to choose seaside fish restaurants, pizza and pasta places, fast food chains, one of the growing number of very good Asian restaurants, or French/international restaurants, where the menu might include a token *tagine* of the day. When it comes to Moroccan food, most people know the best food is prepared in the home.

That said, the medinas of Marrakech and Fes have a number of high quality Moroccan restaurants, often in converted palaces, where a Moorish atmosphere and exquisite dishes offer a memorable evening out. Immaculately costumed waiters serve *pastilla*, *couscous* and *tagines* at low tables, to the strains of classical Andalusian music, perhaps accompanied by a belly-dancer or the tambourines of Berber folk musicians.

In Agadir, Marrakech, Ouarzazate and some of the oases, a few restaurants offer 'Moroccan evenings' in tents. The *caid* tents, laid out with carpets, are traditionally set up for occasions such as *moussems* and weddings. Though rather touristy, such evenings can be fun.

Restaurant Selection

The following list of restaurants stars with those in the main cites and then a selective list of places to eat elsewhere around the country. They have been subdivided into three categories: $$$ = expensive (over 400 Dh per person), $$ = moderately priced (150–400 Dh), $ = inexpensive (under 150Dh).

Agadir *(tel code: 08+)*
L'Amiral, Port de Pêche, tel: 846080. Owned by a former sailor, it serves fish straight from the sea all year round. $$.
Darkoum, Av. du Général Kettani, tel: 840622. Moroccan food with Oriental music and belly-dancing. $$$.
La Miramar, Hotel Miramar, Ave Mohammed V, tel: 840770. Good quality French/international food, with some Moroccan specialities. $$.

Casablanca *(tel code: 02+)*
A Ma Bretagne, Blvd Corniche, Sidi Abderrahmane, tel: 397979. Renowned fish restaurant, on the coast between the Corniche and Sidi Abderrahmane. $$$.
Al Mounia, 95 Rue du Prince Moulay Abdallah, east of Place Mohammed V, tel: 222669. Good quality Moroccan cuisine in oriental setting $$$.
Le Petit Poucet, 86 Boulevard Mohammed V, tel: 275420. Good French food. $$.
Au Petit Rocher, Phare d'El Hank, La Corniche, tel: 366277. Trendy Corniche restaurant and jazz bar. Has excellent view of the Hassan II Mosque. $$.

Port du Pêche, tel: 318561. Popular fish restaurant in the port offering very good value for money. $$.

Fes *(tel code: 05+)*
La Ceminée, 6 Avenue Lalla Asmae, tel: 624902. French-Moroccan cuisine in the heart of the Old Town. $.
La Maison Bleue, 2 Place de l'Istiqlal Batha, tel: 636052. Moroccan restaurant in a renovated *riad* that is also a hotel. Arguably offers the most refined Moroccan cuisine of any restaurant in the country. $$$.
Palais Jamai, Bab Guissa, Fes el-Bali, tel: 634331. Come for its wonderful lunch-time buffet, which is the best hotel buffet in Morocco. $$$.

Marrakech *(tel code: 04+)*
Bagatelle, 101 Rue Yougoslavie, tel: 430274. Closed on Wednesdays. Good French cuisine on a pleasant vine-covered patio. $$.
Le Comptoir, Ave Echouhada, Hivernage, tel: 437702. Fashionable restaurant and *tapas* bar. Attractive modern Moroccan interior. Packed out on weekends. $$$.
Tobsil, Derb Moulay Abdallah Ben Hessaien, Bab Ksour, tel: 444052. Closed Tuesdays. Small and exclusive with great food and an intimate atmosphere. $$$.
Yacout, 79 Sidi Ahmed Soussi, tel: 382929. Renowned Moroccan restaurant in a restored palace. $$$

Dining out in Marrakech
Marrakech's wide range of eateries reflects the presence of a rich expatriate community and its attraction to large numbers of high-spending visitors. It is one of the most exotic destinations in Morocco and is full of eccentric and wonderful restaurants, from the extremely pricey to the very reasonable.

Bars and alcohol

Bars are a late 20th century addition to Moroccan nightlife, and not always a happy one. It's as though they are symbols of the clash between Moroccan Islam, with its traditional rule of total abstinence from alcohol, and Moroccan modernity, with its liberal, Westernised way of thinking. They can be loud and intimidating or furtive and uneasy. Hotel bars are a different matter, and are usually fairly staid. The best bar-life in the country is found in Tangier and Marrakech.

Meknes (tel code: 05+)

La Coupole, corner of Av. Hassan II and Rue Ghana, tel: 522483. Long-established restaurant (founded in 1927), providing a Moroccan and international menu. $.

Le Dauphin, 5 Av. Mohammed V, tel: 523432. Quiet atmosphere; fish is the best-seller. Closed for the religious holidays of Aïd el-Adha and Aïd el-Fitr. $$.

Zitouna, 44 Jemaa Zitouna, by the Parc Zoologique el-Haboul, Bab Tizimi, medina, tel: 530281. Moroccan cuisine served by costumed waiters in a converted Moorish house. Open during Ramadan. $$.

Succulent barbecued lamb

Rabat (tel code: 07+)

Bordj Edddar, Plage de Rabat, tel: 701500. Seafront restaurant specialising in fish. $$.

La Clef, corner of Rue Hatim and Av. Moulay Youssef, tel: 701972. French-Moroccan cuisine on a shady terrace. $.

Dinarjat, 6 Rue Belgnaoui, tel: 704239. Up-market Moroccan *riad* restaurant with floor show. $$$.

Pizza la Mamma, 6 Rue Tanta, tel: 707329. Situated behind the Balima Hotel, this Italian and grill restaurant is deservedly popular. $$.

Tangier (tel code: 09+)

La Valencia, 6 Charih Youssef Ibn Tachfine, tel: 945146. Excellent, no-nonsense fish restaurant, situated up the hill from the beach. $$.

Al-Hoceima (tel code: 09+)

Karim, by the fishing harbour, tel: 982318. Good fish. $.

Chefchaouen (tel code: 09+)

Tissemlal, 22 Rue Targui, tel: 986153. Good regional cuisine. $$.

Erfoud (tel code: 05+)

Café-Restaurant la Jeunesse, 9 Av. Moulay Ismail. Simple restaurant with tasty Moroccan cuisine. $.

El Jadida (tel code: 02+)
Tamaris, Av. Hassan II, tel: 343282. Moroccan and fish specialities. $$.

Essaouira (tel code: 04+)
Chez Sam, Port de Pêche, tel: (04) 476513. Excellent restaurant with relaxed ambience at the far end of the fishing port. First-rate fish. $$.

> ### Nightlife
> The most exciting city at night, and the one with the most Moroccan feel, must be Marrakech, where activity on the Jemaa el-Fna (musicians, magicians, entertainers) can keep going until dawn. Modern nightlife in Marrakech revolves around the nightclubs and casinos, the latter found in the Mamounia and Essadi hotels. The most respectable nightclubs are Paradise (Hotel Mansour) and New Feeling (Palmerie Golf Palace); the Diamont Noir and Stars Club, near the Jet d'Eau roundabout on Mohammed V, are less popular but more accessible. There are many others of varying reputation up and down Ave Mohammed V. Nightclubs in Morocco get going about midnight and continue until 3 or 4am. Entrance tickets cost from 50 to 150 Dh but almost always include the first drink on the house.

Oualidia (tel code: 04+)
Parc à huitres Nr. 7 and **A l'Araignée Gourmande**, the motel restaurant, both specialise in oysters, the town's gourmet speciality. $$.

Ouarzazate (tel code: 04+)
Chez Dimitri, Ave Mohammed V, tel: 882653. This is Quarzazate's oldest restaurant established in 1928 by Dimitri, then a young Greek immigrant. Now run by his son, it is still excellent. Reasonable prices. $$.
Hotel La Gazelle, Ave Mohammed V, tel: (04) 88 21 51. Simple, good quality cooking. $.

La Kasbah, Av. Mohammed V, tel: 882033. Attractive terrace restaurant opposite kasbah. Moroccan cuisine. $$.

Ouirgane (tel code: 04+)
La Roseraie, tel: 439128. Beautiful luxury hotel on the Tizi-n-Test pass through the Atlas. Good restaurant serving international and Moroccan cuisine. Open to non-residents. $$$.
Au Sanglier qui Fume, Ouirgane par Marrakech 42150, tel: 485707. A roadside auberge, which serves homely French cooking. Lunch is served in the garden in summer. $$.

Ourika (tel code: 04+)
L'Auberge de Ramuntcho, Aghbalou, tel: 484521. Slightly more sophisticated alternative to the simple cafés and grill bars. $.

Safi (tel code: 04+)
Le Refuge, 4km (2½ miles) north on the El Jadida road, tel: 464354. Good fish and a view of the sea. $$.

Tafraoute (tel code: 08+)
L'Etoile du Sud, tel: 800038. The speciality is *tagines* with almonds. Served in a *caid* tent. $.

Tetouan (tel code: 09+)
Palace Bouhlal, 48 Jamaa Kbir, tel: 998797. Good *tagines* are the house speciality. $.

> ### Eat like the locals
> On any journey by car, you will come across stretches of highway, often on major junctions, lined with grill restaurants. At lunchtime and in the evening, they are wreathed in smoke and fragrant with the smell of barbecued lamb. The meat is usually of excellent quality (such establishments often double as the local butcher's). For a simple but memorable meal order kebabs, salad and flat Arabic bread.

ACTIVE PURSUITS

MOUNTAIN AND DESERT

There are around 10 summits in the High Atlas range over 4,000m (13,000ft) high. Volcanic ranges such as the Jbel Siroua and the Jbel Sarhro are also well worth exploring.

Trekking tours are led by guides trained in the French Alps and the High Atlas. Porters and mules carry the luggage; basic accommodation is offered in huts, local homes or tents.

Popular departure points for mountain adventures are Asni and Imlil, south of Marrakech *(see panel)*, where arrangements can be made on the spot for ascents of the country's highest mountain, Mt Toubkal (4,167m/ 13,670ft). Travel companies are also expanding into other activities, such as mountain biking and white-water rafting. The latter is possible in spring, when the snows melt, and in late autumn, when the rains fall. Good rafting is to be had on the Dades and Ourika rivers in the High Atlas, and (more demanding) the Oum er Rbia River in the Middle Atlas.

Camel trekking is popular in the desert dunes of the south, with excursions being offered from Zagora and M'Hamid.

The Middle Atlas, with the 2,036-m (6,680-ft) high Mischliffen, and the High Atlas, with the 2,650-m (8,700-ft) Oukaïmeden plateau, are the country's main ski resorts. However, facilities (ski-lifts, pistes, accommodation) are rudimentary compared with those of European resorts. Cross-country skiing is more exhilarating.

GOLF

Hassan II was an enthusiastic golfer and as a result Morocco has some first-class courses. Several national and international tournaments take place here, including the Moroccan Open. There are currently 15 courses and another 18 are planned by the year 2005.

For further information on golf courses in Morocco, write to the Fédération Royale Marocaine de Golf, Royal Golf Dar Es-Salam, Rabat, tel: (037) 755960, fax: 751026.

Climbing Mt Toubkal

The starting point of any ascent of Mt Toubkal or the nearby peaks is Imlil, a lively little commercial centre at the end of the 17-km (10-mile) pot-holed track from Asni. In Imlil it is possible to stock up on supplies, and to hire guides and mules.

The path to Toubkal begins with the hike to Aremd (45 minutes). Here, in the bottom of the valley, is the start of the long, hard slog up to the shrine of Sidi Chamarouch (2 hours), where limited amounts of tinned and packet foods, drinks and bread can be bought, and then up the higher reaches of the Ait Mizane valley to the Club Alpine Français refuge (3 hours), at an altitude of 3,000m (9,840 ft).

The refuge and surrounding ad hoc campsite act as a base camp for climbers attempting Toubkal or any of the surrounding peaks. The normal time for starting an attempt on the summit (3 hours) is around 5.30 or 6am, to avoid the heat and make the top before too much haze obscures the view.

Although Toubkal offers no technical difficulties and the distances are not great for anyone who is reasonably fit, the effects of altitude on the body should be taken into consideration. Add to this the effects of dehydration and sunstroke (the sun is much stronger at high altitude due to the comparative lack of atmosphere), and the dangers of over-exertion become clear. It is wise to take the ascent as slowly as possible and take numerous breaks for drinks to allow one's body to acclimatise.

PRACTICAL INFORMATION

Getting There

BY AIR

Morocco's national airline, Royal Air Maroc (RAM), flies from London Heathrow and most of Europe's other principal cities to Tangier, Casablanca, Marrakech and Agadir. Some of the flights to Casablanca, Marrakech and Agadir involve a stop in Tangier. There are onward flights to Fes, Ouarzazate and other cities from Casablanca *(see page 119)*. RAM direct flights to Casablanca also operate from New York, though not on a daily basis. For further information, contact Royal Air Maroc:

In the UK: 205 Regent Street, London W1, tel: 020-7439 4361.

In the US: 55 East 59th Street, Suite 17B, New York City 10003, tel: 212-750 5115.

British Airways has linked up with GB Airways to run daily flights from London Gatwick to Casablanca (stopping off in Gibraltar), as well as less frequent flights to Marrakech and Tangier. There are also regular flights to Essaouira.

The state railway connects the main towns

Most airports connect to the nearest city by taxi, but Casablanca Airport also has direct rail links with Casablanca, Rabat and Fes.

BY RAIL

From Paris (Gare d'Austerlitz) there is a daily rail service with sleeping cars and couchettes to Madrid, where the train connects with the service for Algeciras, the main port for ferries to Tangier and Ceuta *(see below)*. The complete journey takes up to two days. Morocco participates in the Inter Rail scheme for young travellers.

BY CAR

From Algeciras there are ferries several times a day to Tangier (2½ hours) and the Spanish enclave of Ceuta (1¼ hours). Weather permitting, there are also daily hydrofoil services from Tarifa, a small town west of Algeciras, to Tangier and Ceuta. The Tarifa crossing is shorter and less expensive, but only open to EU passport-holders.

There is also a limited ferry service from Malaga to Tangier and Spanish Melilla. A boat also goes twice a week from Sète (South of France) to

Tangier (36 hours) and in the summer there is a ferry from Sète to Nador (36 hours), in the eastern Rif.

Generally, travelling to Morocco by car is expensive (allow for toll fees in France and Spain as well as ferries and accommodation). For travel through France you will need Green Card Insurance, and for Spain a bail bond, both issued by your car insurers. For insurance in Morocco, it is best to make arrangements at the port when you arrive. A national driving licence is sufficient.

Getting Around

BY AIR

Royal Air Maroc (RAM) and regional airlines, operating from Casablanca, have flights to Agadir, Al-Hoceima, Dakhla, Er-Rachidia, Fes, Marrakech, Ouarzazate, Oujda, Rabat, Tangier and Tetouan. For contact details in the UK and US, *see page 118.*

BY RAIL

Morocco's railway (ONCF) operates an hourly service with air-conditioned fast trains (TNR = Trains Navette Rapides) connecting Casablanca, Rabat and Kenitra, and between Casablanca and the Mohammed V Airport.

Other connections include the west–east route of Casablanca–Rabat–Meknes–Fes–Oujda, and the north–south route of Tangier–Asilah–Rabat–Casablanca– Marrakech.

From Marrakech, the state railway company runs buses to Agadir and into the Western Sahara as far as Dakhla.

BY BUS

Since most people do not have their own cars, buses are the most inexpensive and frequently used means of transport, particularly in the remoter areas. The safest and most comfortable way of travelling is with the privatised

Compagnie de Transports au Maroc, abbreviated to CTM, which operates modern, air-conditioned coaches providing drinks and sometimes films (CTM stations are often separate from the main bus station). There are many other private lines; in the south, one of the best line is SATAS.

A differentiation is made between an *autocar*, a long-distance bus, and an *autobus*, which is a municipal bus.

Taxis

There are three types of taxi: *grand taxi, petit taxi* and *taxi collectif.* The expensive large taxis, most of them Mercedes, go everywhere, whereas the small taxis are only allowed to operate within municipal boundaries (they do not therefore serve the airports) and can take only three passengers. *Grand taxis* and *petits taxis* stop when waved down. The cheap collective taxis supplement the bus service, covering set routes. Rates are fixed and the taxi will not set off until all six places are filled or paid for.

HIRE CARS

Well-maintained cars can be hired from the internationally known agencies, which are well-represented in the larger towns and at the airports. The driver must be at least 21 years of age and have a national or international driving licence.

Most car hire firms require a deposit. It is easier and often cheaper to hire in advance of arrival in Morocco.

TRAFFIC REGULATIONS

Whether the car is your own or hired, always keep the documents – licence and log book – handy to show *gendarmes* (traffic police), who stop motorists frequently, especially at major junctions or on the outskirts of towns. Infringement of the law –

speeding etc – can mean an on-the-spot fine. Speed limits are 50kph (30mph) in urban areas, 100kph (60mph) on the open road and 120kph (74mph) on the motorway between Casablanca and Larache.

The French system of *priorité à droite* (priority to the right) operates. This means that traffic engaged on a roundabout must give way to traffic coming on to the roundabout.

PARKING

Wherever you park in Morocco, there will be a *gardien* (parking attendant), though the centres of some of the main cities are now controlled by parking meters. One or two dirhams is usually sufficient for an hour or two, but overnight parking costs about 10–15 dirhams.

Blatant infringement of Moroccan parking regulations can result in the police attaching immobilising chains to the wheels of your vehicle or removing the number plate.

Tips for the road
The Moroccan road network is well developed and generally in good condition. However, many of the cross-country roads, particularly those south of the Atlas mountains, do not always appear wide enough to accommodate your vehicle and the oncoming car, bus, lorry or fleet of four-wheel drives. In case of doubt, give oncoming vehicles enough room by pulling over onto the verge. You should try to avoid journeys at night, as unlit carts and bicycles, as well as careless pedestrians and animals, are frequently the cause of serious accidents. In addition, what may be marked as a metalled road on your road atlas may not always turn out to be so. A typical example is the route through the Atlas from Anemitèr to Aït Benhaddou *(see page 99)*, which is nothing more than a track and can only be negotiated safely by 4-wheel drive.

Facts for the Visitor

TRAVEL DOCUMENTS
Your passport must be valid for at least three months when you enter the country. British, Irish, Australian, Canadian, US and New Zealand passport holders do not require visas and are normally granted entry for 90 days.

TOURIST INFORMATION
The Moroccan Tourist Board is well represented abroad:
In the UK: 205 Regent Street, London W1R 7DE, tel: 020-7437 0073.
In the US: 20 East 46th Street, New York 10017, tel: 212-557 2520
In Morocco: Every major town or city has a Délégation du Tourisme. The main ones are:

Rabat
22 Av. d'Alger, tel: (037) 730562, fax: 727917.

Casablanca
55 Rue Omar Slaoui, tel: (022) 271177.

Meknes
Place Administrative, tel: (055) 524426. Fès, Place de la Résistance, tel: (055) 623460, fax: 654370.

Marrakech
Place Abdelmoumen Ben Ali, Guéliz, tel: (044) 436131, fax: 436057.

Tangier
29 Bvd Pasteur, tel: (039) 948661, fax: 948050.

Agadir
Place du Prince Héritier Sidi Mohammed, Immeuble A, tel: (048) 846377, fax: 846378.

CURRENCY AND EXCHANGE
There are no restrictions on importing currency into the country. If you

change all your money at the same bank, such as the Banque Marocaine du Commerce Exterieur (BMCE) or the Banque Populaire, you can change it back at the same bank before you leave the country, but you must keep all your currency exchange slips to do so.

The unit of currency is the dirham (Dh), which is divided into 100 centimes. There are 20, 50, 100 and 200 Dh notes and coins of 1, 5 and 10 Dh and of 5, 10, 20 and 50 centimes.

Banks, leading hotels and larger shops in the main souks accept most of the major credit cards. In the large hotels, main stations and the centres of big cities there are currency exchange offices, which are open longer than the banks, though exchange booths in some branches of the main banks (particularly those in popular tourist areas) also keep longer hours. The main cities also have ATMs (cash machines).

CUSTOMS

There are no restrictions on items for personal use. The importing of radio equipment is forbidden and built-in radios in cars are confiscated. When re-entering your own country, every person over 17 years of age has a duty-free allowance of 200 cigarettes or 250g tobacco, 2 litres wine, 1 litre spirits. The import and export of Moroccan dirhams is forbidden.

TIPPING

Leave 10 percent of the bill if you are satisfied with the service in a restaurant. Porters get around 10 Dh.

BEGGING

There are still many beggars on the streets of Morocco. In the main tourist centres, travellers are likely to be pestered all the time. Acknowledged beggars such as the mentally ill and the old or crippled are accorded great respect in Islamic countries and the giving of alms is one of the five pillars of the Islamic faith.

OPENING TIMES

Shops in the New Towns: Mon–Sat 8am–noon and 2.30–6.30pm, closed Sun; the medinas have no fixed hours, and are usually closed Friday.
Banks: Mon–Thurs 8.15–11.30am and 2.15– 4.30pm, Fri 8.15–11.15am and 2.45–4.45pm, closed Sat and Sun; during Ramadan banks close in the early afternoon.
Tourist and post offices: Mon–Thur 8.30am–noon and 2.30–6.30pm, Fri 8.30–11.30am and 3–6.30pm, closed Sat and Sun; during Ramadan, open until the early afternoon.

PUBLIC HOLIDAYS

1 January; 3 March (Feast of the Throne); 1 May; 23 May (national feast); 9 July (birthday of Hassan II); 14 August (Allegiance Day: act of allegiance to Hassan II by the *Sahraouis* in Dakhla); 20 August (exile of Mohammed V); 21 August (birthday of Crown Prince Sidi Mohammed); 6 November (Green March into the Western Sahara); 18 November (Independence Day).

Religious holidays
The dates of religious holidays are determined by the Islamic lunar calendar, which is 10 to 11 days shorter than the Gregorian calendar. The Islamic holidays are thus moveable *(see page 109).*

POSTAL SERVICES

Post offices are marked Poste, Télégraphe, Téléphone (PTT). Telephone boxes are to be found inside and in front of post offices, in stations and often in front of cafés. For longer conversations it is worth buying a telephone card, obtainable in the post offices and at newspaper kiosks. Personally-attended tele-boutiques are also widespread in Morocco.

NEWSPAPERS

International newspapers are on sale at newspaper stands and in the tobacco shops of the large towns and holiday resorts. Among the foreign press, French newspapers predominate.

SECURITY AND CRIME

In general, Morocco is a safe country to travel in. However, in the hustle and bustle of the souks, thefts sometimes occur, so as a precaution deposit your papers and valuables in the hotel safe. What tends to be most intimidating is harassment from *faux-guides* (literally, false guides) who try to force their services on you. The best way to deal with them if you don't want their help is to decline firmly but with good humour. Above all, don't become agitated – it only prompts abuse.

Kif in the Rif

On trips east of Chefchaouen in the Rif Mountains don't stop your car unless absolutely necessary. A stopped car is bound to attract drug dealers, who will try to sell you hashish *(kif)*. Occasionally, cars with tourists are forced to halt by young boys blocking the road: if this happens, keep calm and make it clear that you are not prepared to buy. If you are left with no option, throw it out of the window later.

GUIDES

The tourist police have clamped down on the operation of *faux guides (see above)* in recent years, making it far easier to visit the medinas of the main towns independently. However, this may be only a temporary improvement in what was becoming an intolerable situation. If you find that you are being pestered by would-be guides, or would simply like a knowledgeable local to show you around, hire the services of an official guide, who can be obtained through the tourist office.

CLOTHING

Tidy dress is important for Moroccans. The local people in the medinas and in the country are often offended by people wearing shorts or skimpy tops.

TIME

Morocco keeps GMT all year round.

VOLTAGE

Electricity is 220 and 110V. Travellers from the UK and the US will need an adaptor.

MEDICAL

No vaccinations are necessary for travellers from Europe. Some doctors recommend protection against hepatitis and malaria if you are travelling in country areas. Contact with standing fresh water may carry the risk of bilharziasis. Rabies is present, so take medical advice immediately if you are bitten. Outside the big cities drink only bottled mineral water.

In the towns, medical care is good. Addresses of doctors and dentists can be obtained at the reception desk of large hotels. Travellers are strongly advised to take out a health insurance policy (including repatriation cover), as all medical care must be paid for.

EMERGENCIES

Police (Police secours), tel: 19
Ambulance (Ambulance), tel: 15.
Traffic police (Gendarmerie), tel: 177.

DIPLOMATIC REPRESENTATION

UK: 17 Boulevard de la Tour Hassan, Rabat, tel: (07) 729696.
US: 2 Avenue de Marrakech, Rabat, tel: (07) 762265.

ACCOMMODATION

By and large Morocco's hotels blend harmoniously with their surroundings. Modern architects frequently use traditional elements and incorporate decorative gateways, green courtyards or, in large hotel complexes, Andalusian gardens with tiled paths, marble fountains and pavilions with green-glazed pyramid roofs.

Hotel Selection

As with the restaurants, the hotels for the main cities are given first, and then elsewhere around the country. The selection below is listed according to three categories, each based on a double room with bath: **$$$** = over 750DH; **$$** = 400–750DH; **$** = under 400 DH.

Agadir (tel code: 08+)
Madina Palace, Bvd du 20 Août, tel: 845353, fax: 845308. Extensive Moorish-style complex a few minutes from the beach. **$$$**.
Sahara, Bvd Mohammed V, tel: 840660, fax: 840738. This hotel is an attractive combination of modern and Moorish décor, with a range of apartments and bungalows as well as comfortable hotel rooms. **$$**.

Casablanca (tel code: 02+)
Les Almohades, Av. Hassan I, tel. and fax: 220505. High-quality establishment for guests with high standards, with a stylish Moroccan restaurant. **$$**.
Hyatt Regency, Place. Mohammed V, tel: 261234, fax: 220180. Right in the centre with a view over the city. The bar is the meeting place of the *jeunesse dorée*. **$$$**.
Ibis Moussafir, Place de la Gare, tel: 401984, fax: 400799. Conveniently situated next to Casablanca Voyageurs railway station, this hotel is part of a chain that has been taken over by the French Accor group. The Ibis hotels are modest 3-star establishments, offering value for money and are found in most of Morocco's larger cities. **$$**.
Royal Mansour, 27 Ave des FAR, tel: 313011, fax: 312583. The city's most plush hotel, with an impressive reception area, international restaurant, small rooftop swimming pool and a popular wood-panelled bar. **$$$**.
Safir, 160 Av. des FAR (centre), tel: 311212, fax: 316 514. Caters for a mixture of business travellers, yuppies

The luxurious Mamounia Hotel in Marrakech

and wealthy people. There is a selection of restaurants and the hotel has its own nightclub. $$$.

Maison d'Hotes

Private hotels, or *Maison d'hôtes*, have become very popular alternative accommodation in Marrakech. Rented by the room or the whole house, these hotels – in renovated traditional houses – are usually run by foreign resident owner-managers. They can vary from the super expensive to the very modest in price, depending on size and level of comfort. For the first-time visitor it is advisable to go either on personal recommendation, or via an agency, as there is no effective regulation of such hotels at present and the quality varies widely. Riad agencies include: Marrakech Medina: www.marrakech-medina.com and Riads au Maroc: www.riadomaroc.cybernet.net.ma

---

Fes (tel code: 05+)

Batha, Place de l'Istaqlal, Batha, tel: 634860, fax: 741078, Great-value-for-money hotel, with pool and bar, and possibly the best location of any hotel in Fès. Conveniently opposite the Maison Bleue for dinner. $$.

Maison Bleue, Place de l'Istiqlal, Batha, tel/fax: 740686/741843. One of the original *maison d'hôtes* in Fes. Along with the Riad Bleue hotel (same owners), it offers exclusive family-run accommodation in the medina. $$$.

Meridian Merenides, Borj Nord, tel: 645226, fax: 645225. Completely renovated by the Meridian chain, the Merenides offers a terrace with a famous view over Fes el-Bali and surrounding hills. $$$.

Marrakech (tel code: 04+)

Amanjena, Amelkis, tel: 403353, fax: 403477. Marrakech's most expensive hotel. Located outside town, it is a place to retreat from the world. Archi-tecturally impressive, if a little monastic, it has enormous rooms, hundreds of staff, facilities galore and a price to match. $$$.

Issil, Circuit de la Palmeraie, tel: 309191. Basic hotel, with bar and restaurant. $.

La Mamounia, Bab el-Jdid, tel: 448981, fax: 444660. Wartime leader Winston Churchill came to relax and paint in this super-luxurious hotel. Many other international prominent guests come here to enjoy the winter sun in the 7-hectare (17-acre) Garden of Eden. $$$.

Palmeraie Golf Palace, Circuit de la Palmeraie, tel: 301010, fax: 305050. Moorish-style El Dorado for golfers; pavilions with pyramid roofs, five swimming pools, eight restaurants and golf course. $$$.

Hotel Sherhezade, Derb Riad Zituone Kedim, tel: 429305. Charming family-owned hotel. It is deservedly one of the most popular hotels in the medina. $.

Tichka Salam, Semialia, tel: 448710, fax: 448691. American know-how and Moroccan creativity combine to make a paradise for tourists. $$.

Meknes (tel code: 05+)

Transatlantique, Rue El-Merineyne, tel: 525050, fax: 520057. Fine hotel with a view of the medina. In the large grounds a summer buffet is set out by the pool. $$$.

Rabat (tel code: 07+)

Balima, Av. Mohammed V, tel: 708625, fax: 707450. Centrally located, traditional hotel. $$.

Chellah, 2, rue d'Infni, tel: 701051, fax: 706354. Large modern hotel. $$.

Rabat Hilton, Souissi, tel: 675656, fax: 671492. Not far from Chellah, this hotel serves as the guesthouse of the royal palace. $$$.

Royal, 1 Rue Amman, tel: 721171, fax: 725491. Colonial-style hotel with a view over the Moulina mosque to the municipal park. $.

Splendid, 24, Rue de Ghazza, tel: 723283. Centrally located. $.

La Tour Hassan, 26 Rue Chellah, tel: 704202, fax: 735408. Luxurious hotel in Central Rabat. Part of the Meridian chain. $$$.

Tangier (tel code: 09+)

Continental, 36 Rue Dar el Baroud, tel: 931024, fax: 931143. Located in the medina with an unsurpassed view over the port, the Continental was once Tangier's most fashionable hotel. After a period of decline, the hotel is back on the up with the reopening of its restaurant and a somewhat eccentric redecoration of its rooms. $.

El Minzah, 85 Rue de la Liberté, city centre, tel: 935885, fax: 934546. The best hotel in Tangier and famous for its reasonably priced restaurant, just a short hop from the medina, it offers some excellent views over the bay. $$$.

Tanjah Flandria, 6 Bvd Mohammed V, tel: 933279, fax: 934347. Recommended for those who prefer to do their sightseeing on foot. $$$.

Al-Hoceima (tel code: 09+)

Quemado, by the beach, tel: 983315, fax: 983314. It has rooms and bungalows in the best part of the bay with beautiful panoramic views; only open in summer. $$.

Cascade d'Ouzoud (tel code: 023+)

Riad Cascade d'Ouzoud, tel: 459658. A local house that has been rebuilt and converted into a *riad* (traditional medina house) hotel. Stamped with the friendly personality of its French owner, who will encourage you to discover the superb countryside that lies beyond the famous waterfalls. $$.

Chefchaouen (tel code: 09+)

Hostel Guernica, 9 Onssar, Medina, tel: 987434. An artistic Spanish-run hostel with bags of charm and a pleasant terrace. $.

Parador, Place Makhzen, tel: 986324. Renovated colonial-era hotel with a lovely viewing terrace. $$.

El-Jadida (tel code: 02+)

Palais Andalous, Bvd Docteur de Lanouy, tel: 343745. Former residence of a pacha. $$.

El-Kelaâ M'Gouna (tel code: 04+)

Les Roses du Dadès, tel: 836007. Situated on a terrace above the Asif M'Goun river, a tributary of the Dades. Great views. $$.

Erfoud (tel code: 05+)

Tafilalet, Av. Moulay Ismail, tel: 576535, fax: 576036. The hotel lobby is like a giant desert tent. $$.

Erg Chebbi, Erfoud (tel code: 05+)

Kasbah Dekoua, on the road to the dunes of Erg Chebbi, tel/fax: 577140. Excellent small hotel in the middle of the desert, owned and run by Michel, who wanted to join the Foreign Legion but couldn't pass the medical. $$.

Er-Rachidia (tel code: 05+)

Rissani, on road to Erfoud, by the bridge over the Ziz, tel: 572186, fax: 572585. Attractive garden and swimming pool. $$.

Essaouira (tel code: 04+)

Des Iles, Bvd Mohammed V, tel: 784620, fax: 475422. Large hotel opposite the beach. $$.

Villa Maroc, 10, Rue Abdellah Ben Yacine, tel: 476147, fax: 475806. Exquisitely furnished rooms in two restored 18th-century houses in the heart of the medina. Friendly, intimate atmosphere, good cuisine. $$.

Sofitel Mogador, tel: 479000, fax: 479030. New luxury spa hotel built opposite the beach, with its rooms conveniently arranged around the swimming pool. $$$.

Tafouket, Bvd Mohammed V, tel: 784504, fax: 784505. Basic but very clean hotel. Rooms offer good view of the sea. $.

Auberge Tangaro, Diabat, tel: 785735. Outside the town and with no electricity, but romantic atmosphere and a fireplace in each of the rooms. Half board is compulsory but fortunately the food is excellent. $$.

Midelt (tel code: 05+)

Kasbah Asmaa, tel/fax: 580408. Part of a small, well-run Moroccan chain.

Camping

Camping in Morocco is an excellent alternative to staying in hotels, especially from May until October when the weather can reasonably be expected to stay mostly dry and sunny. Many towns have municipal campsites, which, while varying in facilities and cleanliness, offer secure camping often within walking distance of the centre. Municipal campsites exist in Tangier, Chefchaouen, Meknes, Fes, Agadir, El Jadida and Essaouira to name but a few. Local tourist offices are happy to point out campsites and they are often signposted in towns.

However, camping is at its best out in the countryside, especially in the south with its vast, open, under-populated areas and spectacular scenery. Morocco is a country where you are welcome to camp just about anywhere, and thanks to the honesty and friendliness of the majority of the population, one can do so very safely. If you need to camp in a rural agricultural area, don't be shy to ask a local farmer, who will happily let you set up a tent in an uncultivated field. At most he will ask for a small fee, but will more likely offer you tea and fresh bread to go with your dinner instead.

Modern with local taste in interior design. Friendly and clean. $$.

Ouarzazate (tel code: 04+)

Berber Palace, Quartier Mansour Eddahbi, tel: 883105, fax: 883071. Theoretically the best hotel in town, it is often overrun by large tour groups and cinema crews which puts a strain on the service. Rooms are bungalow-style on the grounds which, if you are unlucky, can mean quite a hike to breakfast. $$$.

Gazelle, tel: 882151. This is an eccentric protectorate-era hotel, with rooms set around a small garden. A haven away from the tour groups. Some regular visitors swear by it; others find that its charm doesn't make up for the fairly basic rooms. $.

Ourigane (tel code: 04+)

Chez Momo, Route d'Asni, Km 61, tel: 485704, fax: 485727. Small new Moroccan hotel set among trees by the river. Has a small pool and an easy-going atmosphere. $$.

La Roseraie, tel: 432094, fax: 432095. Country hotel with garden and swimming pool. Offers equestrian excursions up into the hills. $$$.

Safi (tel code: 04+)

El Atlantide, 50 Rue Chaouki, tel: 462160. In the new town with a view across the medina to the sea. $$.

Skoura (tel code: 04+)

Kasbah Ben Moro, tel: 852116. Kasbah lovingly restored by a Spaniard. A new hotel with a lovely location and a relaxing atmosphere. $$.

Zagora (tel code: 04+)

La Fibule, 6 m du Pond Oued Draa BP/11, tel: 847323, fax: 847271. One of the first Moroccan-owned hotels in Zagora. Friendly, with a pool and location on the edge of the palmerie. $$.

INSIGHT COMPACT GUIDES

Great Little Guides to the following destinations:

Algarve
Amsterdam
Athens
Bahamas
Bali
Bangkok
Barbados
Barcelona
Beijing
Belgium
Berlin
Bermuda
Brittany
Bruges
Brussels
Budapest
Burgundy
California
Cambodia
Chile
Copenhagen
Costa Brava
Costa del Sol
Costa Rica
Crete
Cuba
Cyprus
Czech Republic
Denmark
Dominican Republic
Dublin
Egypt
Finland
Florence
French Riviera
Goa
Gran Canaria
Greece
Holland
Hong Kong
Ibiza
Iceland
Ireland
Israel
Italian Lakes
Italian Riviera
Jamaica
Jerusalem
Kenya
Laos
Lisbon
Madeira
Madrid
Mallorca
Malta
Menorca
Milan
Montreal
Morocco
Moscow
Munich
Normandy
Norway
Paris
Poland
Portugal
Prague
Provence
Rhodes
Rio de Janeiro
Rome
St Petersburg
Salzburg
Shanghai
Singapore
Southern Spain
Sri Lanka
Switzerland
Sydney
Tenerife
Thailand
Toronto
Turkey
Turkish Coast
Tuscany
Venice
Vienna
Vietnam
West of Ireland

UK regional titles:

Bath & Surroundings
Belfast
Cambridge & East Anglia
Cornwall
Cotswolds
Devon & Exmoor
Edinburgh
Glasgow
Guernsey
Jersey
Lake District
London
New Forest
North York Moors
Northumbria
Oxford
Peak District
Scotland
Scottish Highlands
Shakespeare Country
Snowdonia
South Downs
York
Yorkshire Dales

USA regional titles:

Boston
Cape Cod
Chicago
Florida
Florida Keys
Hawaii – Maui
Hawaii – Oahu
Las Vegas
Los Angeles
Martha's Vineyard & Nantucket
Miami
New Orleans
New York
San Diego
San Francisco
Washington DC

Insight's checklist to meet all your travel needs:

- *Insight Guides* provide the complete picture, with expert cultural background and stunning photography. Great for travel planning, for use on the spot, and as a souvenir. 180 titles.
- *Insight Pocket Guides* focus on the best choices for places to see and things to do, picked by our correspondents. They include large fold-out maps. More than 120 titles.
- *Insight Compact Guides* are fact-packed books to carry with you for easy reference when you're on the move in a destination. More than 130 titles.
- *Insight Maps* combine clear, detailed cartography with essential information and a laminated finish that makes the maps durable and easy to fold. 125 titles.
- *Insight Phrasebooks* and *Insight Travel Dictionaries* are very portable and help you find exactly the right word in French, German, Italian and Spanish.

The world's largest collection of visual travel guides and maps

INDEX